INVESTING IN TRAINING AND DEVELOPMENT

INVESTING IN TRAINING AND DEVELOPMENT

TURNING INTEREST INTO CAPITAL

Tony Pont

KOGAN
PAGE

To Gillian . . .
for 25 of the best

First published in 1995
Apart from any fair dealing for the purposes of research or private study, or
criticism or review, as permitted under the Copyright, Designs and Patents
Act, 1988, this publication may only be reproduced, stored or transmitted, in
any form or by any means, with the prior permission in writing of the
publishers, or in the case of reprographic reproduction in accordance with
the terms of licences issued by the Copyright Licensing Agency. Enquiries
concerning reproduction outside those terms should be sent to the publishers
at the undermentioned address:

Kogan Page Limited
120 Pentonville Road
London N1 9JN

British Library Cataloguing in Publication Data

A CIP record for this book is available from the British Library.

ISBN 0 7494 1524 X

Typeset by JS Typesetting, Wellingborough, Northants.
Printed and bound in Great Britain by Clays Ltd, St Ives Plc

Contents

Introduction   1

SECTION A

Chapter 1 What is Training and Development?   7
Definitions   7
A model of organizational structure   9
The role of senior management in training
    and development   12
The role of the line manager in training
    and development   19
The role of human resources in training
    and development   20
The interface between senior management, line
    management and human resources   23
Summary   25
References and further reading   25

Chapter 2 The Organization and Training and
            Development   26
An integrated approach to business and human
    resource development   28
The Investors In People initiative in the UK   35
Case study: Comet Group plc   37
Summary   41
References and further reading   41

Chapter 3 Some Lessons from Psychology for
            Training and Development Practitioners   42
Behaviourism versus humanism   42
Self-actualization: Abraham Maslow (1908–70)   46
Client-centred therapy: Carl Rogers (1902–87)   48
Learning theories that emphasize the importance
    of experience   50
Conclusions – some lessons from psychology for
    HRD practitioners   54
References and further reading   54

Chapter 4 Empowerment and the Learning
Organization: New Concepts for the
21st Century   56
Scientific management   56
The concept of a learning organisation   60
The empowerment concept   64
Does empowerment work? Case study:
  Semco, Brazil.   72
Summary   73
References and further reading   74

SECTION B

Chapter 5 Action Learning   76
What is action learning? A thumbnail sketch   76
Criteria for action learning programmes   77
How action learning compares with traditional
  learning   81
How an action learning set compares with other
  groups   82
Benefits of action learning   83
Types of action learning sets   87
The role of the set adviser   89
Introducing action learning into your
  organization   93
Summary   94
References and further reading   94

Chapter 6 Mentoring   96
What is mentoring?   96
Benefits of mentoring   99
Benefits to the protégé   102
Benefits to the mentor   105
Potential problems of mentoring   106
Steps to implementing a mentoring programme   109
Summary   111
References and further reading   114

Chapter 7 Self-development   115
What is self-development?   115
Why encourage self-development?   116
Management self-development   119

Personal development 121
Career development 131
Summary 134
References and further reading 134

Chapter 8 Counselling and Coaching **136**
Definition of counselling 136
Benefits of counselling 138
The counselling relationship 142
Implementing counselling skills in an
    organization 144
Giving feedback 146
Informal networks 147
Definition of coaching 148
Benefits of coaching 149
Problems in developing coaches 152
The requirements of a good coach 153
Lessons from the world of sport 154
Summary 162
References and further reading 162

Ch_____ ___ _____p___g _____g _____ __ _____ 104
What is training? 165

The role of the trainer 166
Designing a course 167
Preparing for a course 171
Training methods 172
Using visual aids 178
Summary 180
References and further reading 180

Index **181**

Introduction

Training and development is now taking a more centre-stage position in many organizations throughout the world. Either it is receiving a higher profile after many years of neglect, or it is evolving to meet the changing nature of society and organizational life as the workforce of organizations comprises people who were educated entirely after the Second World War and whose expectations differ greatly from their predecessors.

In the USA the American Society for Training & Development celebrated its 50th anniversary in 1994 with its 50th annual and first international conference in Anaheim, California. The USA has seen significant changes and increases in training activities in recent years. Bill Clinton was elected President in 1992 on a platform that pledged greater government support for training and saw the creation in the following year of the Office of Work-Based Learning with the Department of Labor. Its very title indicates a shift of emphasis from previous philosophies and practices with the focus now more on learning than training, and recognizing both the importance of experience and that the workplace itself is a most significant arena for learning and development.

In terms of the development of workplace training, data were gathered from a random sample of 60,000 households between 1983 and 1991 by the Bureau of Census's Current Population Surveys and analysed by the US Department of Labor's Bureau of Labor Statistics. The data related to occupational mobility, job training and length of employment in current post and was summarized by Anthony and Ellen Carnevale in the ASTD's fiftieth anniversary publication. Some significant findings were:

- between 1983 and 1991 all categories of skill improvement training (school, formal company, informal on-the-job and other) increased, with formal company training showing the biggest gain with a 45 per cent increase;
- most of the training was concentrated among workers between the ages of 25 and 44;

- a 48 per cent increase in the number of women receiving training over the eight-year period compared to only 31 per cent for men; and
- the fastest increases in training are occurring among those with the most education.

In the UK, training and development, after years of neglect, began to receive a higher profile from the mid-1980s. The catalyst for change was a series of reports starting in 1985 with the Coopers & Lybrand report, *A Challenge to Complacency*, followed in 1987 with reports from John Constable and Roger McCormick, *The Making of British Managers*, and by Charles Handy, *The Making of Managers*. To those involved in the training and development field, the reports largely confirmed what was already known, notably that:

- British managers received little training in comparison with their counterparts in many other countries;
- most employers committed few resources to training and developing their employees. Whereas German and Japanese companies invested between 4 per cent and 5 per cent of turnover in training, British companies invested between 1 per cent and 2 per cent; and
- no one had any clear idea of what management training should address in order to increase managerial effectiveness.

The reports did much to raise awareness of the deficiency and as their publication coincided with an economic boom in the late 1980s, a greater investment was made by government, employers and employees. Among the changes in evidence was the establishment of regionalized Training and Enterprise Councils (TECs) to replace the Manpower Services Commission (MSC), whose brief was to promote and fund training initiatives in response to expressed local needs. The British Institute of Management (BIM), now the Institute of Management (IM), piloted the Management Charter Initiative (MCI), which defined a number of key competences in an attempt to define what managers actually had to do successfully in order to be effective. Business schools enjoyed an extended honeymoon with a wide range of qualification programmes, most notably the Master of Business Administration (MBA) degree, enrolments for which underwent spectacular expansion.

Whether these various initiatives led to an increase in managerial effectiveness is open to debate. Some undoubtedly did and in some cases a significant improvement in managerial effectiveness was witnessed, allied to improvements to the bottom-line. In other cases any significant improvement or outcome was questionable. What was very much in evidence though, was that the vast majority of employees enjoyed and benefited from increased investment and provision, either by increased job competence or by increased personal satisfaction, growth and confidence. Having tasted from a previously unavailable cup, they wanted to taste more. The demand from employees for an increasing number of training and development opportunities began to escalate and is likely to continue to do so.

Elsewhere in the world the demand for, and provision of, training and development opportunities continues to increase. In the fast growing economies of South East Asia, provision increases; the reasons and emphasis varying between countries. The economically advanced countries of Singapore, Hong Kong, South Korea and Taiwan continue to invest to sustain their impressive growth. The emerging nations of Malaya and Indonesia are increasing their investment to help economic growth. President Suharto of Indonesia was reported in *The Straits Times* on 17 August 1993 as setting the goal of a quadrupling of Gross National Product by the year 2020, with training being seen as a key contributor to the performance required to achieve this ambitious target.

As Europe and the USA begin to emerge from the severe economic recession of the early 1990s the time has come for a significant reappraisal of the training and development field and the contribution it can make to organizational wellbeing. While employees appear to want more and more opportunities for personal growth, organizations which have emerged from an economic buffeting have less cash for investment and certainly less than they had in the late 1980s. On the other hand, organizations that have withstood the economic storms have emerged leaner and fitter than before, but now have to exist in a world of rapid change where increasing international competition is evident and where the pressure is on to show a return on all expenditure. Training and development, as much as any other function, will undergo close economic scrutiny and will have to justify its existence. A case for a return on investment will have

3

to be made. This book will attempt to put forward such a case by suggesting the following.

- Training and development is not just the responsibility of the training department; everyone in the organization from the chief executive to the factory floor has a part to play and this is a collective responsibility.
- Personal training and development needs and the needs of the business are not mutually exclusive, meeting the former can make a significant contribution to the latter.
- The phenomenon of rising individual needs for personal growth can be addressed and can be harnessed for the good of the organization and not just for the benefit of the individuals and at insignificant cost.
- The greatest resource for training and development opportunities lie *within* the organization itself and use must be made of its needs and its employees as a resource for growth and development, both in personal and financial terms. 'People are the greatest resource of the organization' is a much maligned cliché, but it is only true if their knowledge and skills are utilized and their potential harnessed and developed. Five cost-effective ways in which the organization can use its people are discussed in Section B.

The book is divided into two sections. Section B discusses five methods for developing people, using the workplace itself as the arena. Section A concentrates on a number of background topics that have some relationship with the five methods in Section B.

Training and development should be seen as an investment, not a cost, and the interest that individuals have in their own jobs, their organization and their own growth and development should be used to produce greater profits. Profits accumulate to provide capital and the use of employees' knowledge and skills and the development of their potential will provide greater capital and not just capital in the financial sense, but human capital in terms of 'know-how' or expertise. Such reserves will need to be drawn on more and more in the fast-changing times of the 1990s.

The comparison between capital and profit is a useful one in terms of time-scale and an important lesson can be drawn. Profit is short-term whereas capital is long-term. Training and development has often been viewed as short-term rather than long-term and it is important in the years ahead that a more strategic approach be adopted.

A number of 'bolt-on spin-offs' can be derived from training and development activities at little or no extra cost and with a little imagination and commitment. For example, why not use a training and development initiative to receive an award with consequent national and international recognition? It is often said that all publicity is good. Some will doubtless dispute that, but good publicity is surely beneficial for any individual and organization. Ways to gain added-value from training and development activities will be discussed later in the book. This book is not intended to be prescriptive, but to demonstrate that training and development can be seen as an investment, not a cost, and that there exists within every organization enormous resources which need harnessing. I hope it will be thought-provoking and that readers will find something of interest they can implement. Every organization has its own distinctive identity, but all have one thing in common – people – and if some ideas presented here can be adopted and adapted to this common denominator, so much the better. The key word is 'appropriateness'.

Finally, the world of training has changed, not only in response to changing needs, but also in response to changes in knowledge and thinking. Fifty years ago trainers and managers were greatly influenced by behaviourism and Taylorism in how things were done. Since the end of the Second World War new theories and approaches have emerged, some propounded by academics, and these have impacted on the way we think and behave. Nowhere is this more evident that in the fields of adult learning and people-management. Two chapters, therefore, have been devoted to the emerging concepts of the learning organization and empowerment, and to the theories and potential contribution of the humanistic school of psychology. These are not intended to be prescriptive or to form a framework for development, but to be considered and adapted if and when appropriate.

In writing this book I cannot conclude the introduction without a word of thanks to those people who had an influence or made a contribution by giving their time and sharing their ideas and experiences. There is insufficient space to mention everyone, but special thanks are due to:

the numerous managers who have attended programmes, particularly the Action Learning Sets, that I have been involved with in Europe, South Asia and the USA;

Lee Cloete, Management Development Manager, Comet Group plc, for sharing with me developments within the Group and for permission to produce the information on the Group outlined in Chapter 3;

John Malfait, whose work with young cricketers of the Northamptonshire Cricket Association over 15 years demonstrates the progress that good coaching can achieve and who generously gave of his time in granting me an interview;

Edna Pollard, for 20 years of friendship and for typing the manuscript in her usual efficient manner;

Gillian Pont, for making me aware of the power of counselling and for the helpful comments on the manuscript;

Simon and Nicholas Pont for their honest and open feedback and for occasionally providing proof and satisfaction that some of the methods outlined in the book do achieve positive results; and

Jean Whittaker who four years ago persuaded me to begin the explication process which became the catalyst for this book.

It must, however, be stressed that while all the above have been a source of inspiration in their own unique ways, the responsibility for the contents of the book rests entirely with me. I hope the book will stimulate thinking and experimentation and will encourage individuals and organizations to increase their investment in training and development. May the returns be large!

Readers who wish to contact the author may do so at the following address: Heyford House, Manor Park, Nether Heyford, Northants NN7 3NN, UK; Tel: +44 (0) 1327 342339; Fax: +44 (0) 1327 349389.

SECTION A

Chapter 1

What is Training and Development?

'Where shall I begin, please your Majesty?', asked the White Rabbit.
  'Begin at the beginning,' the King said gravely, 'and go on till you come to the end; then stop.' *Alice in Wonderland*

There seems no better place to start than with a definition of the two terms 'training' and 'development'. After that we shall consider a model of organization structure and the roles that senior management, line management and human resources have to play in training and development. And then I shall stop!

Definitions

Many people have seen training and development as inseparable, but a recent report, *Developing the Developers* by Megginson and Pedler (1991) which involved 633 respondents in a survey, found that most managers viewed training and development as different and wanted to keep the two terms separate. The report made the following definitions:

Training: the relatively systematic attempt to transfer knowledge or skills from one who knows or can do to one who does not know or cannot do.
Development: working with individuals or organizations to enable them to cross a threshold which has qualitative significance to them and their life.

7

The term 'Development' is defined further by Margerison (1991) who distinguishes between development at the personal level and at the organizational level:

Personal: the process by which you and others gain the skills and abilities to manage yourself and others. Management development is a personal responsibility.

Organizational: involves all the issues related on a continuum – from recruitment and selection to induction to self-development to top team development. Management development is a way of doing business . . . it is where management development is seen as part of the future, rather than simply solving today's problems that the importance becomes visible to all. In such places you will find a supportive atmosphere conducive to learning.

From these brief definitions a number of very key points arise that need emphasis:

- personal development is a key contributor to the quality of individual life
- *every* individual has a responsibility for development – for self, subordinates and the organization
- training and development should not be viewed as short-term but as long-term; put another way, the emphasis should change from the operational to the strategic
- atmosphere or environment greatly affects learning. Managers need to consider what importance they attach to learning and the kind of learning environment they wish to create.

The notion that training and development is the sole responsibility of the training/personnel/human resources department is outdated and inappropriate. Everyone has a responsibility, although the emphasis, involvement and influence will undoubtedly vary. What the roles and responsibilities are within different parts of the organization need to be considered but before outlining these roles and responsibilities, let us take a general view of the organization.

A model of organizational structure

There are numerous models of organizational structure, but I propose to make reference to the Mintzberg model outlined in Figure 1.1 , which is described in great detail in his book, *Structure in Fives* (1983). While not applicable to all organizations, it can be applied to most, especially those with a manufacturing function. As the title of the book suggests, there are five main parts to the organization.

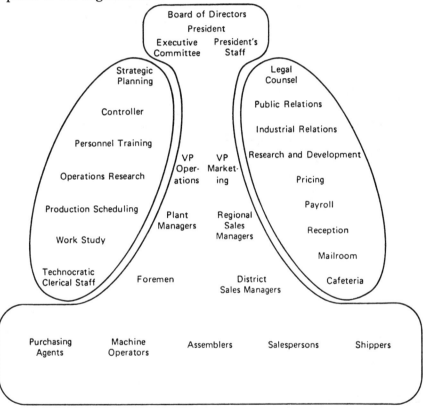

Figure 1.1 *Some members and units of parts of a manufacturing firm, from Henry Mintzberg* Structure in Fives: Designing effective organizations *© 1983, p.18. Reprinted by permission of Prentice Hall, Englewood Cliffs, New Jersey*

1. The strategic apex

This contains the people with the overall responsibility for the organization – the chief executive or president, plus the most senior managers or directors. It is responsible for ensuring the organization serves its mission and that it serves the needs of those who control it and who have power over it, eg owners, government agencies, etc. As a general rule the strategic apex takes the widest and as a result the most abstract perspective of the organization. Work at this level is generally characterized by a minimum of repetition and standardization, much discretion and autonomy and relatively long decision making cycles. Those who form the apex carry out three major groups of tasks.

- Through the middle management they coordinate the work of the organization by such tasks as allocating resources, designing and staffing the organization, agreeing to remuneration packages, authorizing major decisions and so on.
- They monitor and manage the organization's relations with its external environment. This can include informing outside influential people about the organization's work, developing high-level contacts for the organization, serving as figureheads and carrying out ceremonial duties. Senior members of universities are very good examples of the importance of these roles.
- As the body that monitors, watches and hopefully understands the organization's external environment, it is charged with the responsibility of strategy formulation. In this they monitor changes in the external environment and reconcile them with their intimate knowledge of the organization to effect change but at a pace which is manageable rather than disruptive or even damaging.

Strategy formulation and its communication to the organization and its impact upon training and development will be discussed in more detail later.

2. The operating core

This includes those members – the operators – who perform the basic work related to the production of goods and services. Machine operators and sales people are to be found here.

3. The middle line

This forms a chain with formal authority between the strategic apex and the operating core. At the top will be a senior manager and at the bottom will be a supervisor or foreman who directly supervises the operators.

This part of the organization is a crossroads of information channels which flow upwards, downwards and laterally. For example, resources and work have to be allocated downwards; feedback and decisions requiring higher authorization have to be passed upwards; and liaison has to be made with other areas either in the same part of the organization or another part. Thus in a pharmaceutical company, the sales division would have to liaise with its marketing department to ensure that the marketing and sales effort are coordinated; with its production division to ensure that production schedules can meet sales targets; with its personnel division on such aspects as recruitment, employment contracts, exits and so on.

4. The support staff

These are specialized units that exist to provide support to the organization outside its operations. In a university this would include the university press, bookstore and student accommodation. In a manufacturing organization this would cover a whole range from legal services to cafeteria services.

Large organizations tend to provide their own support services instead of purchasing them externally as they can exercise close control over them. This can also reduce the uncertainty of buying them on the open market and perhaps also increase the certainty of the outcome. By fighting its own court cases the manufacturing company closely controls the barristers it uses; and by feeding its own employees in the cafeteria it can control (and even shorten) the lunch break as well as determining the quality of food its employees eat.

The support units are found at different levels of the hierarchy, depending on the receivers of their services. In most organizations, public relations and legal services are located near the top since they tend to serve the strategic apex directly, while at the lower levels are to be found the services with more standardized work akin to the work of the operating core, eg, cafeteria, mailroom.

5. The technostructure

In this area are to be found the analysts who serve the organization by affecting the work of others. These analysts are removed from the operating work flow although they may design it or train others to do it. Thus the technostructure is most effective when it can use its analytical techniques to make the work of others more effective.

The analysts are outside the hierarchy of line management and often fulfil what is termed a 'staff' role. The function of people working in a purely staff capacity is to investigate, research and advise the organization's line managers. They possess no authority to order or command. It is up to the line managers to decide and act accordingly.

It is in this area of the organization that personnel, including training and development, is to be found. IT and administration are also found here. In some organizations the distinction between line and staff functions is not so clear cut and it may well be that staff specialists have line responsibility over their own subordinates. The main difference is that with the line managers they act in an advisory capacity but within their own division or department they possess formal authority over their subordinates.

In Figure 1.2, the personnel director has a staff and line relationship to the managing director on personnel issues, but also has line responsibilities over subordinates in the training, employment, recruitment and health and safety sections of the personnel department.

The role of senior management in training and development

All three of the main duties of senior management outlined in the previous section impact in a major way on the role that senior management has to play in training and development.

- The monitoring, watching and understanding of the organization's external environment and the impact these changes will have on the organization and its employees.

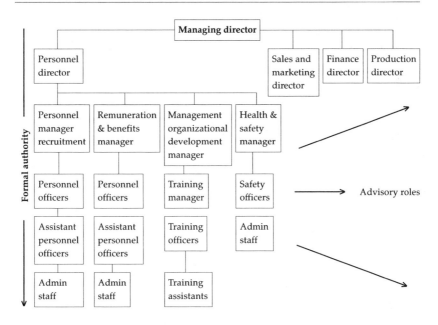

Figure 1.2 *Staff and line relationships*

- The formulation of strategies and its communication down the organization so that training and development needs accord with strategic plans. Training provision can only accord with strategic plans if managers are told what they are! Allied to strategy are a number of other things such as the vision of the future, the mission statement and the business plan, all of which need to be communicated downward. (In order to avoid confusion, definitions of each will be given later in Chapter 2.)
- The authorization of the commitment of resources and particularly money and staff: their commitment will gain the commitment of others. Try selling a management development programme to a company without board approval! Without the cash or management commitment little will happen.

Awareness of the external environment

Through their high-level external contacts and their helicopter view of the world economy (truly the case in the large corporation), senior management must be aware of external trends and continually keep up to date. 'Think globally and act locally' is indeed an imperative.

In the 1990s people are going to be even more crucial to the success or failure of organizations. Herriot (1989) identified five major trends which will be crucial in deciding whether organizations survive the last decade of the twentieth century and emerge fit and competitive into the next millennium. The five trends are as follows.

1. The quality imperative

We live in a global village and the years ahead will see increased competition not only among the industrialized countries of Western Europe and the USA but from the developing world as well. The countries of South East Asia escaped the world-wide recession of the early 1990s and are developing fast. The economies of Korea and Indonesia experienced impressive economic growth alongside that of the established economies of Singapore, Hong Kong and Taiwan. In fact, as stated in the introduction, President Suharto of Indonesia has set a target of a quadrupling of GNP by the year 2010.

Herriot argues that the quality of goods and services will form the basis for competitive advantage, so those organizations making quality and top-priority goods are likely to be successful. In the UK many organizations are now conforming to quality standards set by the British Standards Institute (formerly BS5705) and to more specific industry-related standards, along with international quality standards (ISO 9000). Meeting these standards is, however, merely the start of a journey to continuous improvement and the implementation of a total quality management culture. Such a culture recognizes the importance of the customer, both internal and external, and several organizations have implemented further initiatives beyond the implementation of a quality management system, examples being the Royal Mail 'Customer First' programme and the British Airways 'Putting People First' programme. The new attitude and awareness is demonstrated by the following quotation:

> With the emerging necessity of the so-called 'flat company' will emerge the philosophy that promotes the idea that management must be driven out from the centre of the company to come face to face with the marketplace, divesting itself of

unnecessary, costly layers and supervision and control as it does so.

'Control' in the future must come from the customer, whether that is the internal client dependent on the quality and efficiency of other functions for the satisfactory manufacture of the product, or the ultimate external purchaser. (Sir Colin Marshall Chairman, British Airways, September 1993)

2. The information technology imperative

The growth of on-line data, accessible to all or most in the organization, will improve the quality and speed of decision making at all levels, which will have an effect on the headcount. Information is power so more people will have power and will therefore have greater responsibility. This accessibility of information has already affected the traditional organization hierarchy with 'downsizing' programmes stripping out layers of management. The types of individuals remaining and those recruited will be a different breed from the past and with different training and development needs.

3. The communication imperative

Linked to the growth in information technology is the speed and availability of modern communications. Information on the organization's external environment, now worldwide, is more accessible than ever before. From London, Sydney is as accessible as Surbiton by many communication media. The world's money markets operate on a continuous 24-hour day and satellite TV beams events into our home and office as they happen from the other side of the world. This enables organizations and their employees to be more responsive to changes in a national and international context.

4. The evolutionary imperative

Mergers and take-overs are on the increase. Small and medium-sized companies and occasionally large companies tend to merge or be taken over in the interests of corporate survival. As these conglomerates grow through acquisition they tend to decentralize, creating new divisions and producing different goods and services. A different type of individual with different skills will be required to manage and work in them.

5. The imperative of change

A fast-changing environment requires an organization capable of responding quickly. The traditional bureaucracy, reared in times of steady predictability, is not capable of such quick response and, like the dinosaurs, will slowly perish. In order to survive and succeed, organizations will need to change highly structured controls, long decision making processes and endless discussions in committees to a more responsive structure with fewer layers of management, to become a leaner and more streamlined organization. The Sheehy Report (1993) on the structure of the police force in the UK has recommended changes in this direction.

The speed and extent of these changes has led Kanter (1989) to state that maintaining the old corporate forms will not be good enough to succeed in the future. Instead she says organizations must adopt the four Fs — they need to be focused, fast, friendly and flexible. She says that management must give priority to letting people do what they do best and that any restructuring process must ensure that the organization is able to do 'more with less' rather than 'less with less' so that individual productivity increases. If the process is poorly managed then morale and trust are lowered with a consequent reduction in employee commitment.

The implications of these trends are wide-reaching for organizations and for managers and especially the management of people. It follows, therefore, that the recruitment, training and development and retention of the right people will assume even greater significance in the future.

Formulation of strategy

All managers are involved in the process of planning, but at the senior level the focus is on the planning process with less detail and a longer time-scale and therefore a greater degree of uncertainty and risk involved. The different levels of planning are shown in the table below:

Plans	Time-scale	Degree of detail	Managerial rank
Strategic	5–10 years	Vague	Board level
Management	1 year	High	Departmental heads
Operational	1–2 months	Very high	Junior managers

The overall coordination and implementation of these three levels of planning is called corporate planning. This is concerned with planning for the whole company or corporation in order to ensure that the long-term objectives of each division or department are compatible and do not conflict either with each other or with the overall goals of the organization. The dovetailing of each planning level within the organization is shown in Figure 2.1, in the following chapter.

It would probably be helpful to outline the distinction between corporate planning and strategic planning. Drucker (1968) defined corporate planning as:

> the continuous process of making present risk-taking decisions systematically and with the greatest knowledge of their futurity; organising systematically the efforts needed to carry out these decisions, and measuring the results of these decisions against the expectations through organised, systematic feedback.

Corporate planning defines and clarifies the goals of the whole organization. It involves assessing the organization's strengths and weaknesses and considering the threats and opportunities posed by the organization's environment. All these affect what the organization can realistically achieve. The corporate planning process also involves transforming long-term strategies into more detailed medium and short-term plans to try to ensure the organization's overall objectives are achieved.

The corporate planning system which involves coordinating plans for the whole business or corporation over many years is important because:

- the identified and stated objectives of the organization should be the goal towards which the whole business works, using coordinated strategies. Cohesion is the name of the game. A corporation in which different units have disparate and uncoordinated goals is a recipe for self-destruction;

- all organizations have finite resources and as the organization grows new needs arise and the competition for these finite resources increases. In the last decade, information technology and training and development have become bigger players in the race for a bigger slice of the corporate cake. The need for central planning, coordination and control rather than planning by individual departments, is increased; and

- the ever-increasing pace of change means that organizations have to adapt and react to change on a corporate, not a departmental, basis in order to survive. Strategic planning is the long-range planning part of the corporate planning process. It will involve assessing where the organization wants to be in five to ten years time; where it is likely to be as a result of forecast changes in its business environment; and developing long-term contingency plans in the event that it has to bridge the gap between where it would like to be and where it thinks it might be.

Examples of long-term strategies are the development of new products, the opening up of new markets and the expansion into different areas of business. In the pharmaceutical industry where a new drug may take as long as ten years to come to market, consideration will be given to availability of new products, the cessation of a patent on an existing product which will invite greater competition from generic sources, new forms of an existing product, eg from injection to tablet, or from prescription to over-the-counter sales, and so on. Such long-term planning and coordination is an important role of senior management. The acquisition and development of such skills are a training need in themselves and their communication down the organization must form the basis for training and development activities. This will be elaborated upon in the next chapter.

Committing resources

Senior management, who take a helicopter view of the organization and who gaze into their crystal ball in an attempt to predict and plan for the future, are also in the best position to assess future organization needs and the resources needed in order to meet future requirements.

All decisions to spend significant amounts of money require board approval. It is important, also, that line and staff management perceive that something has the backing of top management, as this is likely to guarantee the commitment of all and potential successful outcomes. Without the backing of top management, any initiative or programme will have limited effect.

The role of the line manager in training and development

But every manager in a business has the opportunity to encourage individual self-development or to stifle it, to direct it or misdirect it. He should be specifically assigned the responsibility for helping all those working with him to focus, direct and apply their self-development efforts productively. And every company can provide systematic development challenges to its managers. (Drucker, 1968)

Nearly 30 years ago Drucker recognized the importance of every manager as a facilitator and enabler of personal development. Since then the importance of the line manager in training and development has received increasing recognition and the AMED report, *Developing the Developers* (Megginson and Pedler, 1991) further emphasized this role.

All training and development activities should be a partnership between the individual (who may well be a line manager), line management and the appropriate human resource specialist. Involvement of all three parties in the contracting, providing and evaluation stages is the name of the game and this is shown diagrammatically in Figure 1.3.

Most managers have their training and development needs regularly assessed through a number of mechanisms, such as a career counselling interview or the annual appraisal process. While the training and development needs of the individual are his or her responsibility, their diagnosis and the meeting of those needs usually emerge as a result of a dialogue and

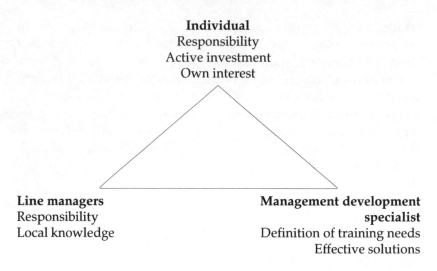

Individual
Responsibility
Active investment
Own interest

Line managers
Responsibility
Local knowledge

**Management development
specialist**
Definition of training needs
Effective solutions

Figure 1.3   *The training triangle*

contracting process between individual and line manager. It is here that the human resource specialist fulfils their staff function by providing appropriate advice, which the line manager and subordinate may act upon. This three-way process should go on at all levels of the management hierarchy.

The willingness of line managers to be involved in this process will vary greatly. Some line managers show a very keen interest; others are less interested and concerned. For many line managers involvement may go well beyond the process outlined. An increasing number of line managers are now becoming involved in the delivery of training itself and are therefore requiring to be trained as trainers. This is one way the organization can utilize its own resources and build up a reservoir of 'know-how' or human capital and slowly orientate the organization towards a culture in which learning is valued. The last chapter of this book is devoted to the acquisition of training skills for new or potential trainers.

The role of human resources in training and development

In the Mintzberg model, the personal/human resources function which often contains training and development people has traditionally been located within the technostructure. In this situation it is peripheral to the main mission of the organization, which can create problems, but it also offers some advantages and can create opportunities. On the one hand it can be seen as an expensive overhead fighting for limited resources with other 'cost' functions and with limited access to or influence on senior management; on the other hand it can stand back and take an objective view of the whole and advise line management (and hopefully senior management too) in a rational and objective way.

Pont (1994) suggests that there are eight major roles for the training and development specialist:

1. *To raise the profile of training and development in the organization.* He suggests that HR has historically suffered from a low profile and lack of political and financial clout. Its input into corporate and strategic planning has been minimal, a situation which is beginning to change as the importance of harmonizing corporate strategy and business planning with training strategy and provision gains increasing recognition.

2. *To market and sell training and development to line management.* The benefits of training and development to line managers and their departments needs selling. The importance of a continual dialogue with line management and working with them as outlined in Figure 1.2 cannot be overstressed. The underlying principle of the quality movement, that we should listen to our internal customers and offer a quality service which adds value wherever possible is very relevant here. In the long term, organizational attitudes change and become more favourable towards training and development through a process of influencing key decision makers of the future.

3. *To assist the creation of a learning organization.* This concept will be discussed in much greater detail later in the book, but a long-term objective must be to create an organizational culture in which learning is accepted as a continuous process whereby individuals are empowered to take responsibility for their own development.

4. *To raise the quality of training and development activities and provide evidence of a return on investment.* For years many training and development activities have focused on inputs rather than outputs, with little direct impact on the bottom line.

Management will, in the future, want to see a return on the investment and therefore, where possible, activities should relate to the organization itself.

5. *To be aware of external developments.* In the same way that senior management should map their external world in strategy formulation, the training and development department should be aware of new initiatives taking place. In the UK in recent years there have been numerous initiatives, often government backed, including Accreditation of Prior Learning (APL), National Vocational Qualifications (NVQs), Business Growth Training (BGT), the Management Charter Initiative (MCI) and Investors in People (IIP). These have all helped raise the profile of training and development and, more importantly in some cases, provided funding.

6. *To design and deliver a portfolio of development opportunities.* There are a whole host of learning and development opportunities beyond a formal course. These include distance learning, job share, swap or rotation, self-development packages, self-development groups, community service, secondment, exchange and so on. A number of such opportunities which are cost-effective are described in detail in Section B of this book.

7. *To develop self and the status of training and development.* The historical legacy of low status and therefore usually low funding has already been outlined. A constant process of influencing key decision makers must be pursued. Some of the ways in which this can be done are through continual dialogue with senior and line management, and demonstration, wherever possible, of the return on investment and the use of the publicity machine both within and outside the organization.

It also needs to be remembered that developers can only develop others if they develop themselves. It is all very well playing the role of nurturing parent taking satisfaction in the development of others, but developers must not neglect their own needs.

8. *To develop consultancy and interventionist skills.* One advantage of being in a staff role with a support function is that one can often apply an external perspective by not being too close to the situation. Distance lends itself to objectivity. The development of consultancy skills is a key skill for human resource specialists as is knowing when to bring in external consultants. The

selection, briefing and managing of external consultants are skills that also need to be developed.

Consultancy resource is often used to assist line management to deal with a situation. A key role for the training and development specialist is to empower line managers through the consultancy process to take responsibility for themselves and their subordinates and to encourage an organizational climate in which this is so. Facilitating the development of the line manager as a developer is crucial.

An excellent example of how this can be achieved, using internal or external consultancy personnel who may work with line managers, is the development of action learning sets. Action learning deals with the reality of the work situation in which managers deal with real-life problems in a realistic time frame and follow a problem through to a solution and implementation. A chapter in Section B is devoted to the use of action learning sets.

The interface between senior management, line management and human resources

In this chapter we have discussed the various roles of these three parts of the organization and the contributions they must make to training and development. The key to success in organizational terms is clear two-way *communication* between everyone. In terms of their interrelationship it is vital that:

- senior management communicate their strategy down the organization, especially to human resources who cannot effectively devise a training strategy, implement training plans and solutions to meet the needs of the business without that knowledge;
- human resources must communicate their needs to senior management, especially the resources required if they are to make appropriate provision. As Margaret Thatcher once said, 'No one would remember the Good Samaritan if he had only good intentions. He had money as well.' The

decision to provide the cash is ultimately made by senior management and persuasive and cost-effective arguments must be presented to them. A key person in this upward communication process is the head or director of human resources who must present this case along with a plea for greater involvement in the strategic planning process; and

• the importance of a continual dialogue between line management and human resources cannot be overstressed. Line management must communicate their training needs so that provision can be made to meet the needs of their department and ultimately the business. In the same way that human resources should be involved in strategic planning, so line management should be involved in training provision. Furthermore, line management can echo the plea made by human resources for greater resources. Decisions in all organizations result from continual influence on key decision makers and human resources should not underestimate the importance of influencing the line to provide additional support for their own political activities.

The interface between the parts of the organization is shown diagrammatically in Figure 1.4.

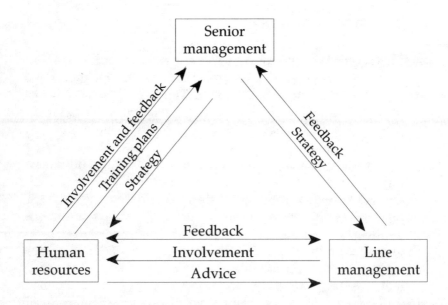

Figure 1.4   *The interface between senior management, line management and human resources*

Summary

Some of the main points from this chapter.

- Training and development needs to be viewed long-term and not short-term.
- Responsibility for training and development rests with senior management, line management and the human resources function.
- Senior management have the key role of mapping the external environment, formulating strategy and committing resources. This must impact upon training and development activities.
- Line managers must take more responsibility and have more involvement in training and development activities. The development of line managers in this role must be encouraged in the future.
- The human resources function, which has traditionally housed the training and development specialists, plays an advisory role and needs to integrate training strategy with corporate strategy.
- Clear communication between the three different parts of the organization is vital to achieve success.

References and further reading

Drucker, P (1968) *The Practice of Management* (2nd edn), London: Pan Management Series.

Herriot, P (1989) *Recruitment in the 90s*, London: Institute of Personnel Management.

Kanter, R M (1989) *When Giants Learn to Dance*, New York: Simon & Schuster.

Margerison, C J (1991) *Making Management Development Work: Achieving success in the nineties*, Maidenhead: McGraw-Hill.

Megginson, D and Pedler, M (1991) *Developing the Developers*, London: AMED.

Mintzberg, H (1983) *Structure in Fives: Designing effective organizations*, Englewood Cliffs, NJ: Prentice Hall.

Pont, A M (1994) The 'role of the management development specialist', in Mumford, A. (ed) *Handbook of Management Development*, Aldershot: Gower.

Chapter 2

The Organization and Training and Development

Where there is no vision the people perish. *Proverbs 29.18*

In the previous chapter the Mintzberg model was used to describe the structure of an organization and the roles and interface between senior management, line management and the human resources division. In this chapter I shall look in more detail at their various roles and how the work of all three should be integrated so that both the organization and its people benefit in the short and long term. In many organizations different parts operate in a vacuum. Communication between the parts is limited so that the work of the parts is not coordinated for the whole. This has often been the case with training and development which has proceeded on an ad hoc basis and has not been integrated fully with corporate strategy and business planning.

The overall aim for organizations should be to ensure that their employees are trained and developed both individually and collectively in order to maximize the contribution made for the organization and particularly to bottom-line profits. The two are not mutually exclusive.

Two problems to date, therefore, have been the failure of organizations, and particularly training departments, to think strategically, and secondly, poor communication between different areas of the organization. Training departments have attempted to rectify a skill shortage when it arose and senior management have failed to develop business plans and, where they exist, failed to communicate them to employees. Consequently, very few employees recognize how they themselves are contributing to the direction of the organization.

Limited research findings in this area reinforce the point. In the UK the Training Agency commissioned a report in 1990 entitled *Skills in Britain*. It covered more than 140,000 organizations with more than 25 employees across all industrial sectors excluding agriculture, forestry and fishing. The report revealed:

less than 48 per cent had a formal business plan
less than 35 per cent had a formal manpower plan
less than 41 per cent had a formal training plan.

Research carried out in 1992 for IBM by Towers Perrin with nearly 3,000 individuals worldwide indicated that this situation is not just confined to the UK. The findings reinforced the point that the HR function should focus more attention on strategic issues rather than operational issues.

This situation has been exacerbated by the fact that the HR function has made relatively little input into the planning process, which has been more the preserve of other functions, notably sales, marketing and finance. This is partly a reflection of the relatively low status that HR has suffered from in the organization, enjoying at best middle-management status.

In terms of developing manpower and training plans, there have been two further problems:

- In some countries such as the UK, personnel professions learnt their trade in the adversarial years of the 1970s and 1980s when trade union influence and power were high and containment and control were the order of the day. Issues relating to growth, productivity and long-term development were not high on the agenda. Strategic or long-term thinking was limited; short-termism and winning the immediate battle were the major concerns.
- In many cases the HR function did not know what the strategic or business plans were, if they existed – communication down from the top of the organization was limited and carefully monitored. Consequently training plans were developed on the basis of a needs analysis focusing on job specifications and job descriptions. By identifying job skills and the gap between the skills required and the skill level of the current job-holder, individual training plans were drawn up.

This situation has been summed up by Darling (1993) who states:

it would seem that very few organisations can claim to have a high concern for strategy and a consistent and integrated approach to training. This recognition of the need to invest in people and develop 'human capital' – as distinct from a short term approach at getting the right people in the right place at the right time – would seem to be light years away.

The advantages of a planned and strategic approach are many and include:

- continued upgrading of skill level so that the gap between current performance and desired performance is reduced
- easier movement of individuals between jobs within the organization
- a valuable and attractive recruitment tool to enable the organization to attract the best people
- reduced recruitment costs because future senior and middle managers are home-grown
- the gradual establishment of a bank of human capital or expertise which is adaptable and competent.

An integrated approach to business and human resource development

Each part of the organization needs to carry out its function and communicate its decisions clearly to other respective parts. The subject of organizational communication is beyond the scope of this book, but the functions of the different parts are not. These were outlined in the last chapter, but will be elaborated upon further, along with an explanation of some relevant terms. Information relating to business and training needs should cascade down the organization and the training department provision should respond accordingly, although hopefully the training department will have made an input into the planning process.

Diagrammatically the process of translating long-term strategic and business planning into training plans should appear as shown in Figure 2.1.

Some of the key terms and how they become integrated into reality will now be briefly outlined.

Figure 2.1 *From vision to provision*

Corporate strategy

This begins with a vision. The top team have a vision of what the future will be like and how the organization will be. Very few people have a clear vision of the future and often those that have are unable to communicate it effectively. The vision will usually become a mission, set out frequently in the mission statement which will usually define what the goal is and how a group of people are going to get there. Two examples of a vision and mission are as follows:

> I believe this nation should commit itself to achieving the goal, before this decade is out, of landing man on the moon and returning him safely to earth. (John Fitzgerald Kennedy, 25 May 1961)

> To be the best airline in the world. (British Airways)

The American nation and British Airways subsequently set out on their mission. Whether British Airways has achieved its mission is not for me to comment, but the American nation certainly did with Neil Armstrong's 'giant leap for mankind' on 20 July 1969.

Once the vision is clear and clearly communicated, a strategy needs to be devised as a move towards realizing the vision. The word 'strategy' is borrowed from the military which, when translated into the business world, involves drawing up a plan to achieve competitive advantage. Examples of a strategy might be to achieve a stock market flotation in five years or to acquire x number of retail outlets in a similar period.

Business development plans

Plans are the means by which strategy is implemented. A good plan will usually address the following:

• what has to be done
• where it has to be done
• when it has to be done
• how it will be done.

The planning process will also involve giving consideration to how potential snags or difficulties will be dealt with; for this, contingency plans will have to be made. A good evaluation system should also be implemented.

In this area a policy statement may be issued. While similar to a plan, it is more general, concentrating more on direction than specific actions. Today, for example, most organizations usually have an equal opportunities policy, and others that are sector-specific, for example a school may have a curriculum policy or sex education policy.

A plan is usually achieved in a series of 'bite-sized chunks' that involve setting objectives to meet targets. There is a degree of overlap between the two, and for simplicity they can be deemed to be the same. These are associated with short time-scales (up to a maximum of a year) and are monitored at regular intervals along the way. Criteria for good objectives setting are represented by the acronym 'SMART'. Objectives should be:

Specific – clearly stating what must be achieved
Measurable – end product can be accurately measured
Attainable – realistic, challenging and mutually agreed
Realistic – relate to the task or personal development of the individual, and have a
Time-frame – have deadlines or completion dates.

Thus the role of the human resources development function (which obviously includes the training department) is to identify the specific needs of the business and deliver a range of provision that is consistent with the vision, mission, strategy and policy of the organization. The role of senior management is to recognize and accept their overall responsibility for training and development and to assist, support and involve the HRD function in their efforts. How the HR function will assess the training needs so that they carry out this role will now be addressed.

Identifying training needs

A thorough training needs analysis (TNA) is a time-consuming job but needs to be researched and conducted thoroughly if training provision is to be cost-effective. Identifying training needs is not just simply a matter of discovering a need and then coming up with a quick-fix solution. There are often conflicting requirements from different interests within the organization. Individual development needs have to be met at the same time as the skill requirements of the organization have to be addressed. All needs, once identified, have to be matched to the appropriate form of training provision.

Needs identification has to balance corporate demands with divisional departmental requirements and with individual requirements. Figure 2.2 outlines a process that balances all these requirements. It shows that corporate strategies should be the umbrella under which individual and organization training needs are identified. This helps to ensure the alignment of training provision with the business direction.

The steps that need to be taken are outlined below.

1. Collect corporate strategies and policies

This is an information-collecting exercise which should be available in company literature. These form the boundaries within which all training and development activities should take place and should be communicated down the organization. If the organization is unclear about its strategies or does not communicate them effectively, this step will have to be missed out and training provision will not completely support the business.

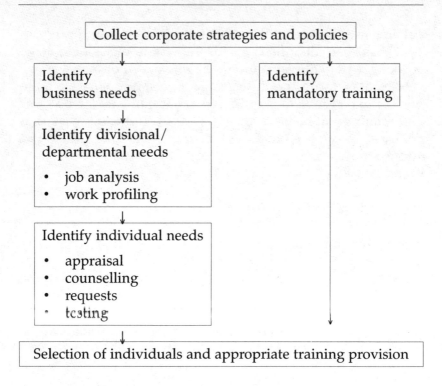

Figure 2.2   *Identifying training needs*

2. Identify mandatory requirements

Company policy will dictate that certain individuals must go on certain courses. This may be as a result of internal decisions or because of a need to comply with legal requirements. Examples of mandatory training are induction training, equal opportunities legislation, new legal requirements and total quality management.

3. Identify business needs

These are usually identified by two main methods: the policy statement and a training forum or steering group.

The policy statement is the means by which the company's strategies are communicated throughout the organization. Each part of the organization then decides *what* it needs to achieve to make its contribution to the company's strategy. The 'what' should be measurable and take the form of goals or objectives.

Once an organization has determined what it has to achieve,

it then has to decide *how* these objectives will be met. Once the 'how' has been identified, it is possible to determine the skills and knowledge the organization will require.

A training forum or steering group consists of a group of training managers and other interested parties who meet to discuss training plans. They also identify opportunities for sharing resources. A forum is particularly useful when there are several, dispersed training organizations within a company. The role of the graph is to:

- provide a 'forum' or stage for identifying an organization's business needs
- ensure that training plans are aligned with the company's direction
- identify opportunities for sharing or exchanging resources.

Line managers should be involved in this forum whenever possible.

4. Identify individual needs

Identifying training needs via business requirements is a 'top-down' approach which ensures that training accords with the business direction. But, with this approach, the coverage is too broad to pick up individual development requirements. Consideration also needs to be given to 'bottom-up' training requests and to ensure both sources of training requirements complement each other. Individual training requirements come from the following sources:

- *appraisal* – an annual event that should agree development needs for the following year and possibly beyond.
- *counselling* – an agreed follow-up to a problem or developmental situation
- *requests* – an individual or manager requests a form of training
- *testing* – can identify a deficiency which can be put right by training.

All of these four sources may have a degree of overlap.

5. Identify departmental needs

As already described, a department's training demands are based on corporate or company business needs and requirements. Individual requirements also help to get an overall picture of departmental needs.

The process for identifying departmental needs is very similar to the process of identifying needs at the corporate level. Each department should assess where it is. The department should have a vision, a mission and a strategy for realizing the vision.

6. Identify skills and training required for each job

Each job has a distinct set of skills and new jobs require new skills. Identifying the training for each job involves:

* identifying the skills required to do a job
* comparing the required skills with the current skills level of the people who will be doing the job.

It is the role of training to bridge the gap between current and required skills. The skills and knowledge required for every job should be well demonstrated along with a record of the kind of training provision that will help a representative person reach the required skill level.

The basis of identifying and recording the required skills is the job description, along with a personal specification. The latter is a profile of the required personal characteristics and skills necessary to do the job competently within a short period of time.

7. Select individuals and provide appropriate training

From the data and information collected relating to corporate policies, mandatory training, business needs, job skill requirements and individual training needs, the training department should be able to identify who will need what training. For example, new supervisors will need training in supervisory skills, new board members may need training on the legal obligations of being a director of a public company, and so on.

It is important that the most appropriate and effective form of training is selected. I have deliberately used the phrase 'training provision' in the chapter and not the words 'training course':

while it is recognized that a course is often the best method of satisfying a training need, there are alternative forms, some of which are suggested later in this book.

The Investors in People initiative in the UK

The Investors in People (IIP) initiative was launched in the UK in 1991 and its purpose is to provide a national standard which will help British organizations get the most out of their people. While predominantly aimed at the business community it has also assisted a number of public sector organizations such as schools and colleges. It requires an organization to make and demonstrate a commitment from the top to develop its people in order to achieve its business objectives. In the first three years of its existence, about 11,000 committed themselves to achieving the national standard.

IIP is based on the results and experiences of a number of successful companies in the UK which have proved that business performance can be improved by adopting a planned approach to setting and communicating business goals and developing people to meet the goals, so that what people can do and are motivated to do matches what the business needs to do.

The key to success is the effective communication of where the organization is going and what is expected, which will mean that people at all levels of the organization should be more involved and make a greater contribution. The national standard has four main principles which are accompanied by a number of assessment indicators. These are relevant to both small and large organizations in the public and private sectors and recognize the individual and unique approach that an organization can take in developing its people.

While IIP is a national initiative, it is administered locally by one of 82 regional Training and Enterprise Councils. The TECs can provide financial assistance for consultancy and administer the assessment process as well as make the IIP award to the successful organization, which is entitled to display the IIP logo on company documentation. Reassessment takes place every three years, so organizations must continue to demonstrate a commitment to developing their people.

The four main principles of the national standard are:

1. A public commitment from the top to develop all employees to achieve business objectives. This will be demonstrated by:
   - senior management developing and communicating to all employees a vision of where the organization is going and the contribution employees will make to its success. Employee involvement in this process is encouraged
   - every employee having a written, but flexible, plan which sets out business goals and targets. The plan considers how employees will contribute to achieving the plan and specifies how development needs will be assessed and met.

2. A regular review of training and development needs of all employees. This will be demonstrated by
   - a clear identification in the business plan of the resources required for training and development
   - managers being responsible for agreeing training and development needs regularly with each employee in the context of business objectives, and setting targets and linking them, where appropriate, to the achievement of the appropriate National Vocational Qualifications.

3. Organizations take action to train and develop individuals on recruitment and throughout their employment. This will be demonstrated by:
   - provision to show how these needs are being met
   - all employees being encouraged to contribute to identifying and meeting their own job-related development needs.

4. Organizations evaluate their investment in training and development to assess achievement and improve future effectiveness. This will be demonstrated by:
   - the investment, the competence and commitment of employees, and the use made of skills learned being reviewed at all levels against business goals and targets
   - the effectiveness of training and development being reviewed by top management, leading to renewed commitment and target setting.

The main benefits of adopting such a planned and strategic approach were outlined earlier and will not be repeated here. In the introduction to the book it was suggested that a number of 'bolt-on spin-offs' could be derived from training and development activities at little or no extra cost and a scheme that is high on the political agenda attracting government backing should be used for all it is worth to assist the organization to obtain an even greater return on its investment or 'added value'. Additional benefits from a national scheme such as IIP are:

- it may offer the organization financial assistance in the form of a grant. Any grant that can help improve business performance and develop people is worthy of consideration. In the case of loans, these may be repayable over long periods at a low rate of interest
- by linking training and development needs and provision with an appropriate qualification, employees get the opportunity to obtain additional recognition for their achievements. By careful planning, the workplace is used as the arena for job improvement, individual self-esteem is enhanced and greater confidence and competence result. It is a good upward spiral of positives
- it offers the organization free publicity. Usually national awards can be used to publicize the recipient. Articles in local or national press, respective trade or professional journals can usually be inserted free of charge; sometimes the writer might even get paid for it!
- the use of a logo that is nationally recognized on company stationery gives out a message which should contribute to the image that senior management wish to give to the world about the organization.

All of these cost very little, but the benefits are considerable.

Case study: Comet Group plc

Starting from humble beginnings in Hull in 1933, Comet has expanded to become a large electrical retailer with outlets throughout the UK. It is part of the Kingfisher group which includes Woolworths, B&Q and Superdrug, and has over 5,000 employees. It recognized that the previously successful 'deal-led' retail culture of the 1970s was no longer appropriate to the demands of the market in the 1990s, and has changed its emphasis to offering total quality to the customer, which includes quality product, price and service. To meet these new, demanding standards, Comet has recognized the need for a well-trained staff who are not only 'efficient, courteous, enthusiastic and committed' but also have the will to continue to develop their skills to meet the ever-changing demands of this competitive retail and service environment.

To coordinate this training and development impetus, a performance management system (PMS) was designed to assist the company to manage and communicate the changes necessary to achieve the business plan. It is a process that establishes a shared understanding of what is to be achieved and how it should be done. The PMS has three stages:

1. *Planning performance* converts thinking about what the company is aiming to achieve into clearly defined performance objectives. A development plan is agreed to support the achievment of these objectives.
2. *Managing performance* is the day-to-day direction and support provided towards the achievement of personal objectives through the implementation of the development plan and appropriate support services.
3. *Reviewing performance* is the final appraisal of performance against what was to be achieved and how it was to be achieved.

The PMS, shown in Figure 2.3, has at its core the company mission and business plan. The process over a year starts and ends with planning, so that plans are continually reviewed and updated in the light of changing circumstances.

The *planning* process begins with managers and subordinates setting objectives, agreeing measures of success and defining training and development needs. An interim progress review date, after approximately six months is set. The *managing* stage is a continual process during the specified period in which progress is monitored against the objectives and the appropriate support provided, either by on-the-job coaching, counselling, or by other more appropriate training and developmental provision. The *reviewing* process begins with an appraisal interview

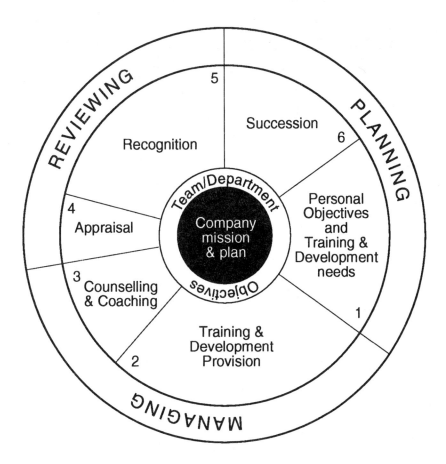

Figure 2.3 *The performance management system*

in which achievements are reviewed against objectives in order to establish an overall performance rating. The appropriate recognition is given, but salary discussions are not yet part of this process. The PMS ends where it began, with the whole process being reviewed and the information relating to performance being used to determine succession plans and planning for the next 12 months.

Part of the appraisal process involves an appraisal of performance against company values because Comet recognizes the importance of not only *what* was achieved, but also *how* it was achieved. Both parties agree a score which best reflects the appraisee's performance, so that low scores could form the basis of a development plan. The five values and their rating scales are outlined in Figure 2.4.

INNOVATION
The desire and ability to generate ideas or make changes to improve performance

A	B	C	D	E
☐	☐	☐	☐	☐
Generates new business opportunities	Seeks solutions/ideas and initiates action	Seeks solutions/ideas to problems	Generates ideas but needs direction	Does not initiate new ideas

CUSTOMER FOCUS
The desire and ability to provide both internal and external customers with a quality service

A	B	C	D	E
☐	☐	☐	☐	☐
Every action/decision has a customer focus	Encourages others to meet customers requirements	Adapts actions to meet customers requirements	Realizes actions have an impact on customers	Does not see job link with customers

TEAMWORKING
The desire and ability to build effective relationships with own team and with others throughout the Company

A	B	C	D	E
☐	☐	☐	☐	☐
Fosters teamworking throughout Company	Contributes to many teams	Contributes a good deal to own team	Contributes a little to own team	Does not contribute to teamwork

LEARNING
The desire and ability to develop oneself and others to improve performance and reach potential

A	B	C	D	E
☐	☐	☐	☐	☐
Sets high standards and takes action to achieve them	Seeks to improve own and others' performance	Seeks to improve own performance	Delivers the minimum required	Low personal standards does not deliver

LEADERSHIP
The desire and ability to enthuse people and gain their commitment towards the achievement of a common goal

A	B	C	D	E
☐	☐	☐	☐	☐
A highly effective leader	Develops others to take ownership and responsibility	Gives direction, delegates and monitors progress	Sets tasks does not delegate	Not applicable does not lead

Figure 2.4 *Company values in Comet*

Summary

The main points in this chapter:

* Organizations need to adopt a strategic rather than an operational stance towards training and development.
* Training and development plans should accord with corporate strategy and business plans, rather than be provided on an ad hoc basis in response to immediate skill shortages.
* Governments often assist organizations in developing their people. The Investors In People initiative, which was launched in the UK in the early 1990s, has attracted a lot of interest and commitment.

References and further reading

Bartram, S and Gibson, B (1994) *Training Needs Analysis*, Aldershot: Gower.

Darling, P (1993) *Training for Profit. A guide to the integration of training in an organization's success*, Maidenhead: McGraw-Hill.

Chapter 3

Some Lessons from Psychology for Training and Development Practitioners

If I keep from meddling with people, they take care of them-
selves,
If I keep from commanding people, they behave themselves,
If I keep from preaching at people, they improve themselves,
If I keep from imposing on people, they become themselves.
(Lao Tsu)

Behaviourism versus humanism

At first glance, the reader may feel this chapter is out of place.
The reason that it has been included is that in the second half of
the 20th century, psychology has come of age as a science and
the contribution it can make to organizational life and individual well-being is being increasingly recognized. This is not
to say that psychology has not influenced these areas in the
past, but as our knowledge deepens and expands and new
schools of thought and theory emerge, the nature of the influence changes and the form of practice changes also. It is some of
the newer schools of thought that are beginning to exert a profound influence on HRD practitioners, most notably in the area
of human growth and development and in the field of adult
learning theory. Ironically, some of the newer schools of thought
overlap considerably with some of the ancient teachings, notably Lao Tsu and Confucius in China, the Hebrew prophets and
Jesus, whose philosophies all emerged from the teaching of
adults. There is unlikely to be anyone who has not been

profoundly influenced by some of the earlier schools of thought in psychology. In many cases, that influence will also have been beneficial. How many of us can claim not to have been influenced by early conditioning in our formative years in junior and high school? How many of us have not come under the influence of scientific management thinking in our careers? And how many of us can say that it hasn't affected our thinking in terms of helping people to learn and developing them for the future?

Many early educational theories, especially those relating to learning, and a number of management theories were influenced by a very mechanistic model in psychology: the behaviourist or stimulus response approach. Famous disciples include Pavlov, Skinner, Watson and Thorndike, and they based their studies on overtly observable behaviours and their measurement. Like Darwin and Freud, the behaviourists saw man as merely another type of animal. Their contributions in many fields, notably learning, were immense and their influence, particularly on our educational system, has been profound.

After the Second World War a new approach emerged in the USA, the humanistic approach, whose exponents often referred to themselves as 'third force psychologists'. Abraham Maslow and Carl Rogers were two of the foremost of these, and they were primarily concerned with the study and development of *fully functioning persons* (to use Rogers' term) or *self-actualizing persons* (to use Maslow's term). They concentrated on the 'inner man' and the quest to achieve potential, taking an holistic approach which holds that the whole is more than the sum of the parts. Much of their work has inevitably focused on the problems and ways of learning. Carl Rogers, a psychotherapist by training, developed the concept of student-centred teaching as a parallel to client-centred therapy. Rogers saw learning as a completely internal process controlled by the learners and engaging their whole being in interaction with their environment as they perceive it.

Some of the differences between the two theoretical approaches, behaviourist and humanistic, are shown in Table 3.1.

In terms of learning the humanists maintain that most human learning is far too complex to be observable, measurable, terminal behaviour. They suggest therefore that objectives might more approximately specify directions of growth such as 'to develop self-confidence', 'to develop a greater knowledge and

Table 3.1 *A comparison of the behaviourist and humanistic approaches*

	Behaviourist or stimulus-response	Humanistic
Nature of human beings	Human behaviour is shaped by environmental forces (reinforcement) and is a collection of learned responses to external stimuli. The key learning process is conditioning	The individual is unique, free, self-determining. Free will and self-actualization make human beings distinct from animals. Present experience is as important as past experience
Nature of psychological normality	Possession of an adequately large repertoire of adaptive responses	Ability to accept oneself, to realize one's potential, to achieve intimacy with others, to find meaning in life
Nature of psychological development	None as such. No stages of development. Different behaviour is selectively reinforced at different ages, but the differences between the child and the adult are merely quantitative	Development of self concept with age, especially self-esteem. Satisfaction of lower level needs are a prerequisite for higher level (growth) needs
Preferred method of study	Experiments in controlled situations (animals and humans)	Experiential
Major causes of abnormal behaviour	The learning of maladaptive responses or the failure to learn adaptive ones in the first place, to distinguish between symptoms and the behaviour disorder	Inability to accept and express one's true nature, to take responsibility for one's own actions and to make authentic choices. Anxiety stems from denying part of self (referred to as identity crisis)
Preferred method(s) of treatment	Behaviour therapy or modification, eg, aversion therapy, behaviour shaping	Client-centred therapy; insights from the client come from the client as present experiences are explored with the therapist
Goal(s) of treatment	To eliminate maladaptive responses and to acquire adaptive ones	To rediscover the whole self, and then to proceed towards self-actualization

understanding of', and so on. Individuals who are systems-ori-entated will doubtless recoil at such ill-defined objectives that are incapable of measurement and evaluation.

This conflict between the mechanistic and humanistic is cur-rently raging in schools in the UK. State schools, which now have to provide a minimum menu called the National Curricu-lum, are subject to educational measurement of the crudest va-riety which has produced a league table of schools based upon examination performance. It takes no account whatsoever of socio-economic grouping, catchment area, special education needs and so on. Neither does it attempt to measure individual development or the progress a child has made over a certain pe-riod of time.

Measurement, whether crude or sophisticated, can be applied to learning, especially that related to knowledge or skill acquisi-tion. Keyboard skills are a good example. But most learning, especially that viewed in a longer-term developmental sense, cannot be reduced to such mechanistic performances. I am sure that many readers will have had experiences where they feel and know that they have developed, but it cannot be measured. This is true in such areas as interpersonal relationships, creativ-ity, analytical ability, sensitivity, judgement and confidence. Thus, anyone connected with HRD must be able to distinguish between the measurement of an end-product which is often a skill, and the individual growth that results from the process which is felt by the individual but cannot be measured by an external source. It is for this reason I have often questioned the usefulness of assessment centres (as distinct from personal de-velopment workshops) where managers attempt to measure complex behavioural criteria or competences with inadequate tools and in so doing detract from the benefits individuals gain by participating in the process. The foregoing has included a number of terms from humanistic psychology that would ben-efit from elaboration, so I will explain these terms in some de-tail. Inevitably, reference will be made to some of the leading exponents in the field.

Self-actualization:
Abraham Maslow (1908–70)

Maslow believed that everyone should have the chance to realize their full potential as human beings. This is an achievable goal because people are basically good, a view which contrasted with those of Freud, who seemed to consider people as being victims of their biological and psychological past. Maslow disagreed, saying that if people's basic needs are met, most of us can live happy and productive lives.

The older schools of psychology were criticized for their negative attitudes towards human nature. Maslow believed there existed a positive and more optimistic picture of emotional life and defined five basic concepts concerning human nature.

- Our essential nature is made up of needs, capacities and tendencies that are good and natural rather than harmful.
- Full, healthy personality development occurs when people develop their basic natures and fulfil their potential. People must grow from within rather than be shaped from without, and unless they do so, they will never reach true maturity.
- Mental illness occurs when people's basic needs are not satisfied, frustrating their inner nature. The role of the counsellor or psychotherapist is to help the client along the pathway of growth and self-knowledge at a pace dictated by the client.
- People's inner nature is weak, delicate and subtle, unlike the overpowering instincts of animals. Although a person's inner nature can grow tall and strong, it begins as a tiny seed. At this stage it can be overcome by environmental pressures, the failure to satisfy basic needs or unhealthy habits. No one's basic goodness ever disappears, even though it may be submerged for periods under self-defeating behaviours.
- As people mature, their potential goodness shows itself with increasing clarity. The self-actualizing person, the fully mature personality, stands out in any environment. Only a very few reach self-actualization, but even those who are making progress towards that level of maturity are recognized and sought after by others.

Maslow developed a hierarchy of needs starting with basic human needs and progressing towards more human needs. Basic needs have to be satisfied before the higher growth needs (metaneeds) can be satisfied. He defined the basic needs as follows:

- *Physiological needs*: the basic need of the human being for food, liquid, oxygen, warmth and shelter.
- *Safety needs*: higher than physiological needs, they are concerned with security and safety from threatening objects or situations. Maslow attached great importance to these in the learning process.
- *Love needs*: the satisfaction to belong to groups (the 'herd instinct'), to receive and give affection and to maintain friendships.
- *Esteem needs*: attainment of acceptable levels of recognition, achievement, competence and confidence in oneself.

Once the basic needs have been satisfied, individuals can strive to attain their metaneeds. Striving to attain these is just as natural for human beings as striving to satisfy basic needs. Maslow defined the metaneeds as:

- *Cognitive needs*: satisfaction of the mind's need to know, understand and explore
- *Aesthetic needs*: the desire to bring beauty and order into one's life
- *Self-actualization needs*: the drive for self-fulfilment; the realization of individual potential ('What a man can be, he must').

As part of his search for a definition of the concept of self-actualization, Maslow studied the lives of a number of successful people. These included Thomas Jefferson, Albert Einstein, Eleanor Roosevelt and a number of personal contacts who demonstrated the qualities of health and creativity that accompany self-actualization.

Maslow discovered that self-actualizing people were able to satisfy their basic needs *and* their metaneeds. They tended to be outgoing, self-reliant, creative and non-conforming and never seemed to allow their problems to be over-bearing. Maslow also discovered that self-actualizing people tended to have more frequent peak experiences or 'Eureka' moments, defined as moments of intense awareness and insight when you feel totally alive, in tune with the world and able to appreciate the beauty and naturalness of the moment. Such moments can come from a variety of sources such as religious experiences or intense participation in an activity. Sportsmen have sometimes related the exhilarating experience of operating at an optimum level of peak performance when mind and body are in complete harmony and new horizons emerge.

Client-centred therapy:
Carl Rogers (1902–87)

Carl Rogers developed a humanistic form of therapy called client- or person-centred therapy, which focused on the client as a person capable of directing their own therapy. He rejected the word 'patient' as he believed it automatically placed the person seeking help in an inferior position. The words 'client' or 'person' imply a partnership in which both parties are equally involved. The therapist's job is to provide understanding, warmth and acceptance. Use is made of a method called non-directive therapy in which the therapist does not attempt to find out what is 'wrong' with their clients, but instead creates a sympathetic setting in which clients find their own path to self-awareness, en route to self-actualization.

Rogers suggests that therapists follow three basic principles:

- Clients receive the therapist's unconditional positive regard. They are valued and respected as people and not judged on their past record. By being shown sympathy and understanding a feeling of trust is gradually engendered, enabling the client to express their feelings openly.
- They do not hide behind their role but appear as genuine, warm, well-adjusted and caring human beings.
- They are non-judgemental and they are not prescriptive. The therapist should reflect back the client's feelings for evaluation and exploration and should help the client arrive at their own solution(s) to their own self-defeating behaviours.

Rogers' non-directive ideas have been widely adopted among counsellors, social workers and others in a helping role. They are worthy of consideration also by managers in such areas as appraisal, giving feedback, career counselling and performance improvement.

Rogers widened his ideas and principles beyond the helping relationship and applied them to the field of teaching and learning. He believed that student-centred teaching is a parallel to client-centred therapy; this approach to learning was based on the following hypotheses:

- you cannot teach another person directly; you can only facilitate his or her learning
- a person learns significantly only those things which are perceived as being involved in the maintenance of, or enhancement of, the structure of self
- experience which, if assimilated, would involve a change in the organization of self, tends to be resisted through denial
- the structure and organization of self appears to become more rigid under threat and to relax its boundaries when free from threat. The individual, therefore, needs to be free from threat in order to learn and so it is important to provide a supportive atmosphere with heavy reliance on student responsibility
- the educational situation that most effectively promotes significant learning is the one in which (a) threat to the learner is reduced to a minimum, and (b) differentiated perception of the field is facilitated; ie, a situation in which individuals obtain the views and perceptions of others in addition to their own will result in greater insight, understanding and learning.

Learning is viewed by Rogers as a completely internal process controlled by the learner who engages his or her whole self in interacting with his or her environment as perceived. Additionally, learning is a natural, life-long process in which the learner will opt for independence rather than dependence along the path of self-actualization and growth.

In the same way that Rogers' non-directive ideas on therapy have been widely applied in other fields, his ideas on learning have many applications in the training and development field. They underpin the methodology used in some areas of classroom and workshop training, self-development activities and in action learning sets, all of which will be discussed in more detail in subsequent chapters.

Learning theories that emphasize the importance of experience

A process model of adult learning

Malcolm Knowles developed a process model of adult learning that differentiated adult learning (for which he used the term 'andragogy') from child learning ('pedagogy'). The model is based around the premise that as individuals mature, their need and capacity to be self-directing, to utilize their experience in learning, to identify their own readiness to learn and to organize their learning around life problems, increases steadily.

Andragogical theory is based on the following four assumptions that distinguish it from pedgagogy or traditional teaching methods:

- *Concept of the learner* – the role of the learner is essentially self-directing and the role of the trainer is to encourage and nurture this self-directed need.
- *Role of the learner's experience* – a learner's experience is accumulated over a lifetime which is a great resource for learning for self and others. Learners attach greater significance to what they experience rather than what they are told. The main training techniques are experiential rather than trainer transmitted.
- *Readiness to learn* – learning should meet the needs of the learner and not be standardized and system-imposed. It should therefore be sequenced according to individual ability and readiness to learn.
- *Orientation to learn* – learners seek to a acquire competence to cope with the demands of their world and they seek immediate rather than deferred gratification. They seek personal development and to achieve their potential.

The andragogical model sees the trainer as a facilitator who helps diagnose learning needs, establish a climate conducive to learning, design a series of learning experiences and deliver or facilitate these experiences with appropriate techniques and resources. The trainer as facilitator is very much in partnership with the trainee and such an approach usually has a profound, positive impact on the learner's acquisition of knowledge and skills, and usually their attitude to learning.

Cognitive Theories

These are an early group of learning theories which relate to the acquisition of knowledge and how to apply it. They have equal relevance for both the child and adult learner, but the application of knowledge is particularly relevant to the latter. They cover the investigative process and the principles of problem solving and decision making, focusing on our internal mental processes.

A key concept of cognitive theory is *insight* which may come from a number of mental processes such as 'understanding', 'thinking', 'reflection', 'analysis of experience', 'memorizing' or 'remembering'. Insight occurs when a solution to a problem becomes apparent, and it is a solution which can be applied in similar or related situations.

The first demonstration of insightful learning was made by W. Kohler in the Canary Islands in the 1920s during experiments with chimpanzees. Bananas were placed at different distances outside the cage beyond the reach of the chimpanzees. Inside the cage and available to the chimpanzees were a number of small sticks which, if slotted together, could be used to reach and procure the bananas. Kohler observed initial periods of exploratory activity which yielded no outcomes, until insight occurred and the chimpanzees solved the problem.

The emphasis therefore, is on the application of existing knowledge to form new insights. We use our internal mental processes to recognize and define problems and seek solutions. Solutions can be achieved by trial and error, by deduction, by seeking information and help, or by a combination of all three. There is, therefore, a greater likelihood that better and quicker solutions can be reached by working in groups rather than solitary working, as was the case with Kohler's chimpanzees. Once the methodology and solution(s) have been internalized, transfer of learning to future situations should occur.

Cognitive theories have been applied in training situations to the technique of discovery learning and problem solving. With this technique, the trainee, upon being given a task has to search and sift clues on how best to progress. A means of unassisted learning through experience is provided that will hopefully lead to the development of insights into key relationships and solutions. Cognition theories have much in common with more recent experiential learning theories which underpin many management training and development programmes.

Experiential Learning

This relatively recent theory puts the emphasis on the actual experiences that people go through as the starting point of the learning process, and then emphasizes the mental processes that individuals use to analyse the experience. Feelings are also part of any experience which, if explored and analysed, can help increase self-insight. In short, experience when allied to analysis can bring about behavioural change.

Experiential learning theory was developed in the 1970s by David Kolb, who said that learning follows a cycle and that there are four distinct stages in the learning cycle. The cycle was modified in the 1980s by Peter Honey and Alan Mumford (see Figure 3.1) who linked the four stages in the cycle to help explain four individual differences in learning style. Awareness of individual preferences in learning style is an important prerequisite in learning how to learn.

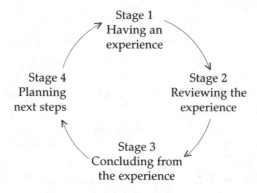

Figure 3.1   *The Honey-Mumford learning cycle*

The cycle begins with an experience which the participant will reflect upon, then make conclusions, before entering a fourth stage in which the participant will test new concepts and ideas to see if they work in practice. The cycle begins again with implementation of the new ideas.

The four learning styles relate to the four stages in the cycle, as follows:

a preference for the activist style – equips you for stage 1
a preference for the reflector style – equips you for stage 2
a preference for the theorist style – equips you for stage 3
a preference for the pragmatist style – equips you for stage 4.

Activists are usually extrovert individuals who learn best from activities where they encounter new experiences/problems/opportunities. They enjoy the here-and-now and love to 'have a go'. Routine and longer-term consolidation have little appeal.

Reflectors prefer a more back-seat role, standing back and observing. Good at data collection, they like to conduct a thorough analysis before reaching a conclusion. Cautious, they do not like pressure and tight deadlines.

Theorists are good at relating experience to existing models, concepts, theories and systems. They like to be stretched intellectually and prize logic and rationality. Usually possessed of analytical skills, they are frequently most effective operating in a detached position on the edge of events.

Pragmatists are practical, down-to-earth individuals who look to implement at the earliest opportunity what has been offered. Their motto is, 'if it works, it's good'. The focus is very strongly on implementation and output.

Most people have distinct learning style preferences and the development of the styles, especially a broadening of the range of learning styles, can form a very useful self-development exercise.

Experiential learning theory also underpins a method now increasingly used in management training and development, named 'action learning'. This method was pioneered by Revans in the UK with such organizations as the Coal Board and GEC, and it utilizes the group as a resource for solving real-life, work-related problems. More will be said about action learning, self-development and learning to learn later in the book.

Conclusions – some lessons from psychology for HRD practitioners

As a science, psychology has come of age and the lessons for practitioners are many. The two theoretical approaches, behaviourism and humanism, outlined in this chapter tell us that:

- You can have measurable returns on many HRD activities but do not make a god out of measurement. Many measurements have considerable shortcomings which need to be recognized.
- HRD activities can be provided by many means. They need to be viewed as long-term, not short-term, and many activities with a heavy emphasis on process cannot be measured in clear, meaningful, quantifiable terms. However, it is possible to provide activities with (a) measurable returns and (b) individual growth, with such activities as action learning projects.
- The human being is a unique individual with an intrinsic need to develop self. The role for the HRD practitioner and line manager is to provide the means and the framework to capitalize on this self-directing need for development.
- Managers will increasingly be taking a helping role, particularly in such areas as appraisal and career development. The adoption of a person-centred approach in coaching, counselling and mentoring can bring great benefits and dividends to those involved.
- We should never underestimate the role of experience in designing learning and development activities.

By utilizing individual interest in self, we develop human capital for the organization.

References and further reading

Heider, J (1986) *The Tao of Leadership*, Aldershot: Wildwood House.
Honey, P and Mumford, A (1982) *A Manual of Learning Styles*, Maidenhead: McGraw-Hill.

Honey, P and Mumford, A (1986) *Using Your Learning Styles* (2nd edn), Maidenhead: McGraw-Hill.

Knowles, M S (1975) *Self-directed Learning*, Chicago, IL: Association Press/Follett.

Kolb, D A (1984) *Experiental Learning*, Englewood Cliffs, NJ: Prentice Hall.

Maslow, A H (1968) *Towards a Psychology of Being*, New York: Van Nostrand.

Rogers, C (1961) *On Becoming a Person*, London: Constable.

Chapter 4

Empowerment and the Learning Organization: New Concepts for the 21st Century

It is my hypothesis that the present organisation strategies developed and used by administrators (be they industrial, educational, religious, governmental or Trade Union) lead to human and organisational decay. It is also my hypothesis that this need not be so. (Chris Argyris 1985)

In the previous chapter, the focus of attention was on the emerging field of psychology and how the emphasis and influence had changed away from behaviourism to a more humanistic approach. This chapter will focus on the changes that have taken place this century in the organization of work and learning at work. The focus will not be on the structure of work or organization, but on the rationale underpinning job design, the execution of work and the relationship between work and learning.

Scientific management

One of the major 20th century influences on the design of work was Frederick Taylor (1856–1915) whose principles of scientific management or 'Taylorism' were first published in 1911 and were widely applied in many organizations and still have a profound influence today. Taylor was an engineer by training who had an obsession with control, which influenced his thinking. He advocated five simple principles for work design, which are as follows.

- All responsibility for the organization of work should be removed from the worker and given to the manager. Managers should think, plan and design work, and the workers should carry out the prescribed task.
- Scientific methods should be used wherever possible to determine the most efficient way of getting the job done. Time and motion study can be used so that the worker is told the precise way in which to carry out the task.
- Select the best person to do the job.
- Train the worker to carry out the task efficiently (using stimulus-response techniques as part of the conditioning process).
- Monitor and evaluate performance to ensure procedures have been followed and the desired results achieved and make adjustments as appropriate.

Taylor's ideas were widely adopted and led to significant improvements in productivity in many industries such as car production. Such improvements were achieved at great human cost, as many workers were reduced to automatons. The needs of the individual were subjugated to the needs of the organization and all training was designed to ensure that individuals did not think for themselves, but could fulfil their prescribed role in an efficient way.

Such a mechanistic approach has distinct advantages in some fields and there have been spectacular success stories. It is appropriate,

- when a simple, straightforward task has to be performed
- when a standardized product needs to be produced repeatedly
- in a stable world with little change so that the demand for the product is predictable
- when the worker is compliant and conforms to instructions and regulations.

This method has been most successful in the application of mass-production techniques; today many of the tasks which were previously carried out by humans are performed by robots. It also underpins many bureaucratic procedures and has influenced the design and working of quality systems that seek ISO 9000 approval. Assessment and consequent certification is largely achieved by the auditing and inspection of the system and its paperwork, rather than the individuals who operate the system. Some cynics might even suggest that scientific management has affected some educational systems in that prescribed content, methods and processes produce standardized results and products!

A modern-day spectacular example of success using scientific management principles is the McDonald's fast food chain. As a parent I have patronized their outlets worldwide on a regular basis, safe in the knowledge that for a modest sum enormous appetites will quickly be satisfied by a product of guaranteed quality. A 'Big Mac' in Hong Kong, London or San Francisco, looks and tastes the same. Why? The constituent parts and the processes relating to their preparation are carefully prescribed and standardized in the detailed application of 'hamburger science'. McDonald's has made a success out of imposing a 'carbon-copy bureaucracy' worldwide, offering a product and service that clearly meets customer needs.

A mechanistic approach can have a number of limitations. It creates and perpetuates large organizational forms (usually bureaucracies) which are slow to adapt to changing circumstances. It encourages, and often rewards, mindless and conformist behaviour. Subservience to the system is expected and any innovation or creativity is usually discouraged. Often those who question and challenge conventional practices are viewed not as innovators, but as troublemakers who are either coerced into conformist behaviour or shown the door. Those who remain often display apathy, concentrating on avoiding mistakes rather than displaying initiative. In the long term, they become institutionalized, passive and totally dependent on the organization, which acts as provider and safety net. Any change can create a severe life crisis as individuals lack the coping skills and inner reserves to adapt. Examples of this institutionalized dependency and problems of re-entry are patients returning to the world after a period of hospitalization and servicemen returning to 'civvy street' after a career in the military.

A mechanistic approach can also encourage competition rather than collaboration between different parts of the organization. This is especially so when limited resources are available and success is usually achieved at the expense of others as a result of influence or political clout. This competition is fostered by the fact that individuals perceive their world within the confines of their job or department. They do not take a helicopter view of the world or the organization and consider only achievement within their area. This manifests itself in selfish and irrational behaviours such as empire-building, careerism, pet projects or whims, all of which may be beneficial to a part of the organization, but not to the whole.

Scientific management can also provide the framework for the safeguarding of individual psychological needs which are at the expense of the organization. In the same way that the organization can exercise control through mechanistic procedures, so also can the individual. The bureaucracy can be a comfortable arena for individuals to satisfy their own needs by allaying their insecurity fears. Like Taylor, many people have a high need to control, and managing through the imposition of strict procedures and regulations greatly reduces personal threat. This is because mechanistic procedures and organizations can ensure that life will hold fewer surprises, that events will pursue a more predictable and safer path, that the status quo is maintained and that any challenges to position can be reduced, minimized or nullified. Many an employee has left an organization due to the frustration of lack of recognition, either because they were not given the opportunity to reveal their talents or were effectively muzzled to minimize their impact. The loss to the organization in terms of future talent may be huge and beyond calculation.

The mechanistic approach to work design tends to limit rather than fully utilize human abilities present within the organization. Individuals are moulded to fit the requirements of the role required rather than moulding the job to the strengths of the individual. In short, talent is under-utilized and potential is not given the opportunity to flower. Both employer and employee lose in this situation: the individual suffers from stunted personal growth and is denied self-actualization: the organization fails to capitalize on the contribution its employees are capable of making. Learning and development is much reduced.

Bureaucracies learn slowly – not only because they stunt the growth of their members, but also because even when members in the periphery learn, their knowledge is ignored when decisions are made. Thus a bureaucracy is often less intelligent that the people in it.

The intelligent organizations of the future are learning networks. (Elizabeth and Gifford Pinchot 1994)

Mechanistic organizations developed in an age when the mechanization of life was a part of a broad social trend. Much of the education and training influenced by behaviourism and Taylorism was geared not to helping people think and understand, but to make them fit and fulfil the requirements of the job so the organization could proceed along a predetermined and predictable path. In this environment, learning and work were largely separated – individuals attended an external course before returning to work in order to perform the job more efficiently. Learning and work were usually separate and rarely integrated.

As we move from a machine age to one based on information technology and new principles of organization, attitudes to learning and work are changing. With new technology, new attitudes and thinking, learning is re-entering the workplace and being integrated into all aspects of work, from applying new technology, becoming more customer-orientated, making continual improvements and restructuring the organization in response to changing circumstances. All these changes are being implemented by an involved workforce who are using the experience of their everyday work to improve individual and organization performance in the drive for continuous improvement. In a more enlightened age, organizations will be made up of individuals and teams and these will be learning and adapting to change as part of a continual process.

The concept of a learning organization

The view of organizations as machines which dominated thinking in the 1950s and 1960s is being replaced by a view of them as organisms or living systems interacting environmentally with other organisms. If an organization is a living entity in which both the parts and the whole can learn to change, then individuals perceive some similarities with themselves in that they can learn and influence each other for the benefit of both.

The learning organization concept is a relatively new one; there is no hard and fast definition, nor is there an organization which can be held up as a shining example. One definition is:

'One which facilitates the learning of all its members and continuously transforms itself as a whole' (Pedler *et al.* 1991). This implies an organizational climate in which individual learning is encouraged and the organization as a whole is capable of learning. It has developed the 'learning habit', learning not only from its actions, but also from the process of taking action; which is a continuous process.

As far back as 1969, Revans described a learning company when he outlined the characteristics of 'the enterprise as a learning system'. According to Revans (1982):

> We observe that all expert systems here referred to must now be imposed upon the enterprise from above or from outside. But action learning must seek the means of improvement from within, indeed from the common task... the daily round offers constant learning opportunities.

Like the client-centred counsellor or the self-directed learner, Revans sees the use of the organization's inner or own resources as the means to solving problems and implementing solutions.

Revans identified five significant characteristics of a learning company:

1. that the chief executive places developing the enterprise as a learning system high among his own responsibilities;
2. maximum authority for subordinates to act within the field of its own known policies that become known by interrogation from below;
3. codes of practice and regulations are seen as norms around which variations are deliberately encouraged as learning opportunities;
4. any reference to what appears an intractable problem to a superior level should be accompanied both by an explanation of why it cannot be treated where it seems to have arisen and a proposal to change the system so that similar problems arising in future could be suitably contained and treated; and
5. persons at all levels should be encouraged, with their immediate colleagues, to make regular proposals for the study and reorganization of their own systems of work.

Exactly how action learning works and how it can be used in an organization will be described in Chapter 5.

More recently, Senge (1990) has focused on the learning organization concept saying that in the future successful enterprises will be those that develop a capacity for sustained organization-wide learning. This is not easy to achieve. Senge suggests that a learning organization should exhibit the following capacities:

* the ability of everyone to continually challenge prevailing thinking and learn from experience. Questioning the status quo and received wisdom is essential to learning;
* the ability to think systematically (to see the big picture and to balance the long- and short-term consequences of decisions);
* the ability to build shared visions that capture people's highest aspirations. Shared vision is vital for the learning organization because it provides the forms and energy for learning; and
* the ability to use the creative capacity of the team to create the outcomes its members want.

Such organizational capabilities are rare, states Senge, for two main reasons. First, they require new individual attitudes and skills that are poorly developed. The influence of behaviourism and Taylorism in formative educational years and early career has been profound, so that very few people have developed the ability to learn how to learn or have developed the survival skills to operate outside of the old world of hierarchies and procedural controls. The emerging world of flatter structures, independent cost-centres or networks is unknown, and is both threatening and frightening.

A second reason is that organization and individual learning are different. As individual capabilities for learning develop, so will organizational capabilities and the latter will require a critical mass of individuals operating in new ways so that new organizational norms and habits are established. The learning habit will become established slowly and learning will become embedded in the organization's culture.

In moving towards the creation of a learning organization, training and development personnel have a number of key roles to play, notably:

- the design and facilitation of learning activities. In a learning organization more and more learning events will be the responsibility of line management who will need to tap the expertise of training and development professionals in order to deliver the goods. In other words, organizational learning is provided and supported by line management and training and development specialists as a *partnership*
- to diffuse new learnings throughout the organization. It is important that learning from all activities is diffused throughout the organization for the benefit of all. Learning from experience should be recorded and shared and those who have benefited from a particular experience given the opportunities to advise others when appropriate. The catalyst in this whole process should not be line management but training and development specialists.

A glimpse into the future

As we move to an age dominated by information technology, humanism and the global village, and in which change is the norm, the way we think about work will change dramatically. Writing in the ASTD's 50th anniversary publication, *A Monstrous Opportunity*, Davis and Botkin (1994) suggested that a number of old phrases and concepts will be replaced by newer ones, as follows:

Old	New
trainee	learner
employee	performer
continual change	transformation
quality improvement	process re-engineering
hierarchies	many organizational forms
the transfer model of learning	the social model of learning
training events	self-directed learning on the job
big training departments	out-sourcing training
monoculturalism	diversity
the invention of new training technology	the application of training technology
big companies	small companies
individual workers	teams
functions	processes

leadership	stewardship
control	empowerment
local	global
school-age education	lifelong learning

The empowerment concept

Along with the concepts of the learning organization and total quality management, empowerment is very much a late 21st century concept and contrasts sharply with the thinking prevalent in the 1950s and 1960s. So what exactly is empowerment? It inevitably means different things to different people, but there do appear to be a number of common themes in existence and these will be described and elaborated upon by reference to the existing body of knowledge. Some of the common themes relating to the empowerment concept are:

- helping individuals assume greater responsibility for themselves and their job. This includes responsibility for personal growth and self-actualization;
- freeing people from unnecessary rules, regulations and procedures that limit their responses to situations and constrain their actions. This will decrease the response time to customers whoever they may be;
- enhancing the contribution individuals make to their team and the organization as a whole, so the organization utilizes more fully the potential of its employees; and
- fostering and developing an organizational climate and culture in which greater personal responsibility and decision making is encouraged rather than suppressed. Greater responsibility for this is passed *down* the organization, to be placed in the hands of those who are closest to the situation and/or the customer. Power is therefore transferred in varying amounts from management to employee in the long-term interests of the organization as a whole.

Stewart (1989) states:

This trend away from exercising power based on position and towards using the personal kinds seems to be the new direction of corporate America . . . . Real power comes from giving it to others who are in a better position to do things than you are. The idea behind sharing power more broadly is to move decisions as closely as possible to where action can be taken.

Such a complete devolution of power down the organization will not happen overnight. Many individual managers will be reluctant to let go of the power and control that more traditional management systems allowed. Therefore a move towards an 'empowerment culture ' must be viewed long term rather than short term and many organizations will take the process forward step by step to maintain their comfort level. Organizations will therefore be at different stages in their journey.

What empowerment is

Bowen and Lawler (1992) suggest three types of empowerment, as follows.

1. *Suggestion involvement.* This is a small shift away from the control model. Employees are encouraged to contribute ideas through formal suggestion mechanisms or quality circles, but their everyday work activities do not alter. The power to decide whether to implement suggestions remains with management. At its worst it is lip-service to employee involvement; at its best it is employee consultation.
2. *Job involvement.* This is a significant departure from the control model. Jobs are redesigned to enable employees to use a variety of skills, often their strengths. Instead of the person being moulded to the job, the job is partly moulded to the skills of the individual. Employees see their job as significant and relevant to the direction of the organization, have considerable autonomy in deciding how best to do the work, and receive more constructive feedback from all directions than employees in a control organization where usually feedback is only given when mistakes are made. Despite this increased empowerment, employees do not input into high-level strategic decisions which remain the prerogative of senior management.
3. *High involvement.* This is virtually the mirror image of a control-orientated organization. Such organizations give *all*

employees a sense of involvement, not just in how they do their jobs but in the whole organization's performance. Information relating to all aspects of the business performance is shaped vertically and horizontally throughout a flattened (de-layered) organization. Employees develop, largely through practice, wide-ranging skills in teamworking, problem solving and decision making and are usually involved in some form of profit sharing and employee ownership.

Such a level of empowerment does exist and has sometimes achieved impressive results in terms of business performance. Examples are Federal Express in the USA and Semco, Brazil; reference will be made to the latter later in the chapter.

Like TQM, heading in the direction of empowerment is a continual journey, but it should not be the goal of every organization. All forms of empowerment are not suited to every organization, and the degree of empowerment must be dependent upon circumstances. Nevertheless, as a practical and productive way to tap into the potential of yourself and your staff, which is often grossly under-utilized, it merits careful consideration. Implementation should be a gradual process, backed by appropriate support systems and training opportunities.

What empowerment is not?

A quick read of the foregoing section could possibly encourage managers to jump on the empowerment bandwagon, seeing it as a way of dumping personal responsibility on others, or increasing individual workloads as part of a cost-cutting exercise by reducing the head count. To elaborate further, empowerment is not any of the following.

1. *Delegation*. Delegation requires subordinates to be given both responsibility *and* authority to encourage the initiative of subordinates enabling them to develop. Often the subordinate is given responsibility for the task but no authority to carry it through. Letting go of both responsibility and authority can prove threatening for managers, because they lose an element of control of the situation. Feelings of inse-

curity can be increased for managers if subordinates successfully carry out tasks, because it makes it less easy for managers to cling to the myth of their indispensability. Furthermore, this myth may be reinforced by the behaviours of the subordinate who wishes to avoid being delegated to.

Empowerment goes beyond delegation, although it may well exacerbate rather than alleviate the feelings of insecurity of managers. Oates (1993) says that whereas 'delegation is actioned by the manager, empowerment, if it works well, is actioned by the subordinates'. The necessary support will, though, be provided by the manager, as in the delegation process, through periodic monitoring. Thus a manager who is an enthusiastic advocate of empowerment is one whose primary concern is helping subordinates grow and develop, rather than controlling them efficiently.

2. *Dumping and/or cost-cutting*. Defined as 'the indiscriminate assignment of work to others', dumping is neither delegation nor empowerment. It is often associated with a cost-cutting exercise by getting others to take on the work of a member of staff who has left, or to avoid taking on a replacement, either temporary or permanent. Staff are usually fairly quick in realizing that they have been 'dumped on', so motivation and commitment beyond the short term is usually a problem, particularly in a buoyant labour market.

Why do we need to empower?

If we have progressed satisfactorily since the early 18th century through the industrial revolution to a point in time in which the onset of the second millennium is imminent, why do we now need to empower? The control model and distinct and large hierarchical structures have served us well for centuries, so why do we need to change? The control model and the hierarchy will no doubt continue to exist in various forms, but the world of work in which they are to be applied is changing beyond recognition. Some of the main reasons why empowerment requires serious consideration as a medium- and long-term strategy are outlined below at the individual, managerial and organizational levels.

Individual

People are now viewing personal development and job expectations very differently to their predecessors. In the UK, the post-war 'baby boomers' are now approaching their half century and occupying positions of significance in public and organizational life. Many of these come from the ranks of what was dubbed the 'meritocracy' – those who had access to higher education in the 1950s and 1960s on the basis of merit, not ability to pay. These individuals see learning as a lifelong process, one that does not decline with age; that the boundary of human potential is unknown; and that personal development is important for individual satisfaction and occupational success. Members of this generation are also viewing occupational success, not strictly in terms of hierarchical progression but in other terms such as personal development and intrinsic satisfaction. In the past five years, many of this generation have suffered from down-sizing or delayering operations and realize that in future they will have to operate outside the security of an organization and probably as part of a wider network (possibly international). Empowering themselves to develop the self-confidence and skills of self-reliance to operate in this new, threatening but challenging environment is an important goal.

At the same time, the sons and daughters of the 'meritocracy' are now progressing through the higher education system and emerging to take their place on the job market. Thus for the first time ever in the history of British society, both the senior, middle and junior ranks of the working population are staffed in significant numbers by those with experience of and qualifications from higher education whose levels of expectations in terms of job aspirations and personal development are high.

A similar scenario probably exists in many of the countries of the West. The generation born in the 1960s has been dubbed 'generation X' in the American novel of this name by Douglas Coupland (1994) who states that this generation view personal development as more important than money, power or even comfort at work. Professor John Hunt of the London Business School, in an extensive research project (1993) with a sample of over 20,000 managers, found that attitudes among managers had changed over the past two decades. Whereas in the 1970s power was the most important motivator, in the 1990s autonomy and independence had risen in importance, with the acquisition of new skills of great importance among 'generation X'. This new generation are also much less prepared to accept the old command and control systems of the past, prizing a job as a development opportunity or means to an end, rather than an end in itself. Every job must be milked as a development opportunity because the trend towards more freelance working or short-term contracts means that people must use every opportunity to increase their portfolio of skills to make them more marketable for the next opening. The individuals who will do well in the years ahead are those with a wide and varied portfolio of skills.

This trend towards lifelong learning is reinforced by surveys in the USA. Information gathered by the Bureau of the Census's Current Population Surveys in 1983 and 1991 from a random sample of 60,000 households was analysed by the US Department of Labor's Bureau of Labor's Statistics. Among a wealth of data analysed, two trends are significant:

- 48 per cent more women received training in the 1991 survey than in the 1983 survey, compared to a 31 per cent increase for males; and
- the fastest increases in training are occurring among those with the most education. Those with some college experience or with college degrees experienced increased skills improvement training on the job between 1983 and 1991 – by 52 per cent for those with some college experience and by 49 per cent for those who gained a degree. Skill improvement training among employees with high school education or less increased by only 23 per cent over the same period.

Self-empowerment is not a quick, easy fix, but is a continuous process. Individuals cannot be empowered by others but must empower themselves. Also, we cannot empower others if we do not empower ourselves. Personal empowerment depends on the kind of messages we send ourselves. If we develop a positive internal dialogue our perception of the world and how we behave towards it are very different from that which a negative internal dialogue produces. The messages we give out are picked up by others and their behaviour frequently reflects ours. Ways to develop a positive self-image are explored later in the book.

Managers

The biggest concern for managers is that empowerment will weaken their own position in that they lose control of a situation, the security of the rule book is not there to back them up, and their authority is undermined by the power their subordinates have taken. But this may not necessarily be the case and in fact, empowered managers can strengthen their position.

Aileen Stewart (1994) distinguishes between a manager who is *an* authority and one who is *in* authority. The latter has traditional authority from role or position whereas the former is an empowering manager to whom staff can turn to for advice, help, support, etc., when the need arises. Credibility and status come from recognized expertise which the manager has worked to develop. Empowered managers require different skills from those traditionally associated with the older forms of management, which required a thorough knowledge of the rule book which was relatively easily learned and could often compensate for managerial inadequacy. The new style requires far more complex skills, particularly interpersonal skills, the acquisition of which is a continual process and can be achieved through numerous developmental activities such as counselling, coaching, mentoring and training, all of which are discussed later in the book. Empowerment makes greater, not lesser demands on managers, but it is also more rewarding. The analogy can be made with training or teaching in that the safest and easiest method is to lecture from the podium from where the trainer can control everything, as opposed to facilitating a group where the degree of control is small, the unexpected frequently arises, but the satisfactions can be far greater.

So what does an empowered manager do? What distinguishes them? An empowered manager:

- is a disciple of McGregor's Theory Y (people desire responsibility and self-management), believing that people want to do a good job and will focus on helping them perform rather than on preventing them from performing. As Peters (1994) states, 'It is impossible to get people's best efforts, involvement and caring concern for things you believe important to your customers and the long term interests of your organisation when you write policies and procedures that treat them like thieves and bandits';

- is a facilitator rather than a director of tasks; one who devolves power down the line to where it is most needed, giving the individual personal responsibility and authority for the work;
- doesn't just talk about empowerment, but actually takes steps to make it happen;
- is people-orientated and enjoys helping people grow rather than controlling them efficiently with procedures;
- devolves power to staff and has the confidence in self to 'let go';
- fosters creativity, questions and challenges the status quo, and supports initiative;
- projects a positive self-image and is committed to self-development; and
- encourages similar commitment in others, providing resources as and when appropriate.

This list is not exhaustive, nor is the following list summarizing the change in thinking regarding the work of a manager that has taken place over the course of the 20th century. On the left are the more traditional roles declared by Fayol (1916); on the right are some of the roles fulfilled by an empowered manager:

Traditional managers	Empowered managers
plan	enable
organize	facilitate
coordinate	consult
control	coordinate
	collaborate
	support
	develop and, most importantly,
	communicate.

To acquire the skills of an empowered manager requires greater investment in training and development by individuals, managers and organizations. The organization itself can be the most important and relevant resource for this process.

Organization

The biggest single overhead of any organization is its employees, yet most staff if asked (and if they answer honestly) would say they are not working to full potential. The most expensive overhead is the most under-utilized resource because many organizations drown their people in rules, regulations and procedures designed to prevent them using their initiative rather than using their own discretion and making a decision on the spot. Customers, who provide most of an organization's revenue, complain they can never get an instant decision at the point of contact, and must wait for approval from above. Is it surprising that staff become demotivated and demoralized and customers become dissatisfied? The penny is slowly dropping and organizations are beginning to wake up to the situation, although much of the change in attitude has been forced upon them by recessionary pressures resulting in considerable delayering and down-sizing. It is beginning to dawn on organizations that:

- they need to make greater use of the potential of their employees. As one CEO said, 'We finally figured out that for every pair of hands we hire, we get a brain for free. So why not use it?'
- they need to develop those brains, using the workplace itself to maximize the return on their greatest overhead. As Peters (1994) states, 'Value added through brains is, simply put, the only strategy'.

Does empowerment work?

Case study: Semco Brazil

An increasing number of organizations have started the journey to empowerment, some with spectacular success. Perhaps the most spectacular example is the Brazilian company, Semco, which is based in Sao Paulo and manufactures industrial equipment such as pumps and cooling units. At a time of world recession and national hyper-inflation, Semco introduced a company-wide empowerment programme that saw a five-fold increase in profits in real terms and a seven-fold increase in productivity. The instigator of the empowerment programme was the company President, Ricardo Semler, who prefers to call himself 'counsellor'. The programme has seen the following.

- A reduction in management layers from 12 to 3 so that a rigid, hierarchical structure has been replaced with a flatter structure reporting to the centre.
- A staff reduction in the personnel department from 45 to 2, along with a 75 per cent cut in staff in the legal, accounting and marketing functions and the elimination of data processing, training and quality control departments. This was because Semler believes that functions such as personnel have been created in response to line managers' failure to solve their own problems.
- Everyone in the company has access to company information and shares in the decision-making process in all areas, including future strategy, site layout, salary levels, profit sharing and choice of up-line manager.
- The implementation of a 360-degree appraisal system in which everyone is appraised twice a year by colleagues, subordinates and boss with focus on long and short term.
- The out-sourcing of many services.

In a recent survey, 93 per cent of the workforce said they were well-motivated and wanted to come to work. This, along with the impressive bottom line results, has brought Semco and Semler international recognition and persuaded many other companies to consider and adopt a similar approach.

Summary

Some of the main points of this chapter.

- The design of work and jobs in the 20th century was greatly influenced by the principles of scientific management which were well suited to certain organizational forms and types of job. They often do not encourage individual development and are often inappropriate for new forms of organization such as networks in a world of rapid change.

- As we move into the 21st century, information technology will have an increasingly dominant impact on work, and the workplace itself will become a significant arena for learning.
- Organizations will become 'learning organizations' in which learning is part of the culture, and individuals who comprise these organizations must become more competent at learning to learn. Training and development specialists will facilitate these developments and need to actively involve all levels of management in the process.
- In a world of rapid change and flatter organizational structures, and in order to utilize more fully the potential of their employees, organizations will have to entrust greater power and control down the organization to those who are closest to the job and the customer.
- In the future organizations will have to provide greater opportunities for personal development, as all generations of employees will be committed to the principle of lifelong learning.
- Empowered managers will fulfil many different roles from those displayed by more traditional managers schooled in the control and command approach.

References and further reading

ASTD (1994) *The Past, Present and Future of Workplace Learning,* Alexandria, VA: ASTD.

Argyris, Chris (1985) *Strategy, Change and Defensive Routines,* London: Pitman.

Bach, Richard (1978) *Illusions,* London: Pan.

Bowen, D E and Lawler, E E (1992) 'The empowerment of service workers: what, why, how and when', *Sloan Management Review,* Spring, 33, 3.

Clutterbuck, D and Kernhagan, S (1994) *The Power of Empowerment. Release the hidden talents of your employees,* London: Kogan Page.

Cook, S (1994) *Training for Empowerment,* Aldershot: Gower.

Coupland, D (1994) *Generation X,* London: Abacus.

Davies, R and McDermott, O (1994) *45 Activities for Developing a Learning Organisation,* Aldershot: Gower.

Davis, S and Botkin, J (1994) 'A Monstrous Opportunity', in *The Past, Present and Future of Workplace Learning*, Alexandria, VA: American Society for Training and Development (ASTD).

Fayol, Henri (1916) 'Administration Industrielle et Générale – Preyvoyance, Organisation, Commandement, Co-ordination, Contrôle', in *Bulletin de la Société de l'Industrie Minerale*. Reprinted in Henri Fayol (1949) *General and Industrial Management*, translated by Constance Storrs. London: Pitman.

Foy, N (1994) *Empowering People at Work*, Aldershot: Gower.

Garratt, B (1987) *The Learning Organization*, London: Fontana.

Hunt, J W (1993) *Work Interests Schedule Norms*, London: MTS.

McGregor, D C (1960) *The Human Side of Enterprise*, New York: McGraw-Hill.

Oates, D (1993) *Leadership: The art of delegation*, London: Century Business Books.

Pedler, M J, Burgoyne, J G and Boydell, T H (1991) *The Learning Company: A Strategy for Sustainable Development*, Maidenhead: McGraw-Hill.

Peters, Tom (1994) in 'The Future of Workplace Learning and Performance' in *The Past, Present and Future of Workplace Learning*, Alexandria, VA: American Society for Training and Development (ASTD).

Pinchot, Elizabeth and Gifford (1994) 'The Future of Workplace Learning and Performance, in *The Past, Present and Future of Workplace Learning*, Alexandria, VA: American Society for Training and Development (ASTD).

Revans, R W (1982) *The Origins and Growth of Action Learning*, Chartwell Bratt: Bromley.

Semler, R (1993) *Maverick!*, London: Century.

Senge, P (1990) *The Fifth Discipline: The art and practice of the learning organization*, New York: Doubleday/Currency.

Senge, P (1994) *The Fifth Discipline Fieldbook: Tools, techniques and reflections for building a learning organization*, New York: Doubleday/Currency.

Stewart, A M (1994) *Empowering People*, London: Pitman.

Stewart, T A (1989) 'A user's guide to power', *Fortune*, 6 November.

Taylor, F W (1947) *Scientific Management*, London: Harper & Row.

SECTION B

Chapter 5

Action Learning

There is no such thing as a problem without a gift for you in its hand. You seek problems because you need their gifts.

(Richard Bach)

What is action learning? A thumbnail sketch

Action learning is probably one of the most challenging ways to develop people within an organization. It is challenging for both developer and for those being developed. It puts everyone on the line, especially human resource and training personnel, so it is a forward-thinking and self-assured person who dares to introduce action learning into an organization.

It is totally earthed in reality. It involves groups of real managers in real organizations working on real issues and problems that have no obvious answers. It focuses on what really matters to managers at the time and it guides them towards learning to ask themselves and each other the type of intelligent and probing questions that will enable them to come up with effective solutions to their problems. The solutions reached may not be the right solutions to the problems and this is why group or set members are often referred to as 'comrades in adversity'.

Action learning sets are similar to quality circles in that the solutions require changes to be made in the organization, which poses challenges to senior management. An element of risk is therefore involved but the benefits are great because people own their problems and their solutions. As a philosophy, action learning is organizationally led, but each organization that adopts this approach must evolve its own particular brand of how it can work in practice. The training and development specialist therefore plays a crucial role in this process, often working with sets to support them in the appropriate fashion. Without doubt, action learning is a dynamic approach to management development and an increasing number of business schools are using the approach in a range of qualification programmes. Such development is long term and it can provide the vehicle for implementing real change in the organization. It is not just the latest flavour of the month, but has been well tried and tested. It was first pioneered by Revans in the coal mines of Britain in the 1940s, but has since been used widely on numerous programmes throughout the world.

Criteria for action learning programmes

Action learning programmes are usually directed at the managerial level. Some are purely organization-related, while others can gain added value for participants by being linked to an action learning management qualification. For both the focus is on the participants' reality, notably their job or an allied job, and relates to their own organization. Action learning programmes must have the attributes discussed below.

Sets

A set is a group of managers who assemble and meet regularly. The set focuses on real problems and seeks solutions within a realistic time frame.

According to Revans (1982), a definition of learning is depicted by the equation

$L = P + Q$, where
L = learning
P = programmed knowledge ('the stuff of traditional instruction')

Q = ability to ask the right questions at the right time and taking action.

In action learning sets the level of P, programmed or existing knowledge, is insufficient to solve the problem or problems facing the set. It is by asking questions and obtaining answers from whatever source available that the body of knowledge, or P, is added to.

Two major sources for obtaining knowledge are (a) the appropriate use of external specialists/experts who are invited to set meetings to provide an input; and (b) the individual set members, who may provide an input and therefore add to existing knowledge using their own experiences or expertise.

A set is usually composed of between ten and 15 managers. Beyond 15, problems of coordination emerge and even at this number sub-sets often emerge in order to assist set management. At set meetings members must be freely able to criticise, support and advise each other without rancour – but this is not always the case. Sets sometimes function extremely effectively, sometimes ineffectively.

In an action learning set, set members increase their knowledge base, but perhaps more importantly, learn more from the process of working, questioning, analysing, deciding and learning together. Process is as important, if not more important, than content; 'how' is as important as 'what'. If both are internalized and transferred to the workplace, extremely effective learning results.

Projects

At the outset a real problem must exist in a real time frame which is of significance to the set members' organization. This becomes the project. There are four major action learning choices, which are shown in Figure 5.1.

Both tasks and situations are subdivided into 'familiar' and 'unfamiliar'. Examples relating the four situations could be as follows:

Box 1 – familiar task, familiar situation: a production manager or supervisor undertakes a project in their own area.
Box 2 – familiar task, unfamiliar situation: an accountant in the

Task		Situation	
	Unfamiliar	Doing an unfamiliar project but in a familiar work situation ③	Doing a project in another organization on a new task ④
	Familiar	Doing a project in an area you know well ①	Doing a familiar task but applying it to a new situation ②
		Familiar	Unfamiliar

Situation

Figure 5.1 *Types of action learning projects*

finance department may undertake a project in another department, for example working on a compensation and benefits package in personnel.

Box 3 – unfamiliar task, familiar situation: a head of department who is part of a senior management team may have to undertake an unfamiliar task with that group. For example, a college of higher education may wish to review its admissions policy and a senior manager would head the project.

Box 4 – unfamiliar task, unfamiliar situation: an example would be chief executives and a board of directors who would be concerned with policy and strategy formulation.

These examples illustrate the fact that action learning can be an appropriate method of learning at *all* levels of the organization. At the higher levels or strategic apex of an organization, managers monitor the external environment which is less under their control and therefore represents a large amount of the unfamiliar. Unfamiliar tasks and unfamiliar situations tend therefore to be more the preserve of top management but the same principles in action learning terms still apply.

Clients

An organization-related project requires a client who is ultimately the person who will make the set member accountable for the project. The client owns the problem, wants a solution and ideally should be in a position of authority to implement the recommendations, or at least to influence those who can implement. Thus for many managers, involvement in an action learning programme is an opportunity for them to raise their own profile within the organization.

Set adviser

This is an individual whose task is to facilitate the learning process. The set adviser is not a teacher who imparts knowledge at regular intervals to passive set members, although occasionally he or she may be the source of expert knowledge. The set adviser role is crucial to the success of the set and a section will be devoted to it later in the chapter. In organizations this role may be taken initially by human resource specialists who may also train line managers in facilitation skills and build up a pool or bank of expertise. In some situations, an external consultant is used; this is often the case with action learning sets involving senior management. On business school programmes, either qualification or non-qualification, the set adviser will

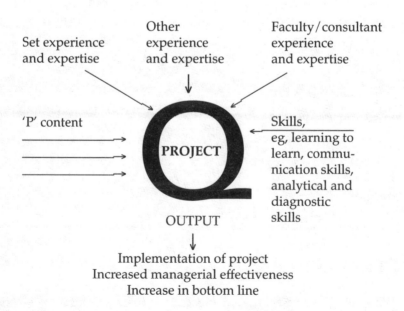

Set experience and expertise

Other experience and expertise

Faculty/consultant experience and expertise

'P' content

PROJECT

Skills, eg, learning to learn, communication skills, analytical and diagnostic skills

OUTPUT

Implementation of project
Increased managerial effectiveness
Increase in bottom line

Figure 5.2 *Inputs and outputs of an action learning project*

usually have some relevant specialist knowledge in addition to relevant life experience and process skills.

Diagrammatically, an action learning programme can be summarized as in Figure 5.2.

How action learning compares with traditional learning

Action learning will be an uncomfortable experience for managers who:

- have been conditioned by didactic teaching in large, passive groups
- were educated in, and believe in, a system that rewards memory, not understanding
- believe learning is a solitary occupation
- like knowledge for knowledge's sake
- work in a highly structured, hierarchical system in which they have learned appropriate responses related to role
- do not like to risk themselves.

Margerison (1989) believes that the philosophy of action learning is essentially existentialist, meaning that 'Action Learning pursues the further understanding of people and projects. We are not studying something at arms length, but rather arm in arm. We study it in order to change for the better'.

Revans (1982) refers to the process as 'system gamma', which involves 'the symbiosis of a person changing a situation (action) and of the person being changed by this action' (learning). To understand what this philosophy means in practice, Margerison contrasts the traditional approach to learning with the action learning approach:

Traditional Learning	*Action Learning*
Historic case studies	Current real cases
Individual orientation	Group-based learning
Learning about others	Learning about self and others
Studying other organizations	Studying own organization
Programmed knowledge (P)	Questions (Q) plus P

Planning	Planning and doing
Arm's length	Arm in arm with client
Input based	Output/result based
Past orientated	Present and future orientated
Low risk	Higher risk
Passive	Active

How an action learning set compares with other groups

A set is a unique entity, with a limited life span, dedicated to solving problems and implementing solutions. By putting the action into learning, set members learn by participation; and by putting the learning into action the outcomes of the set are implemented. Working with or in an action learning set is different from other groups, as explained below.

Team – a team is usually assembled to work together on *one* particular task, hopefully through to completion. A set is formed to work on the problem for future action by each set member.

Course or seminar – this usually has a shorter life span and usually receives prepared presentations and handouts from a tutor or visiting speaker whose role is clearly defined. The content of the seminar will not usually relate fully to the world of the participant – it will be somewhat removed from the participant's reality – whereas a set meeting focuses on the individual's own reality. Courses, and certainly one-off seminars, are much more structured and less spontaneous and the presenter does not receive feedback for implementation (other than perhaps on teaching style!) in their real world. In other words, there is little measurable output.

Formal meetings – a set does not have formal agendas and pre-scribed roles. It does not vote and discussion focuses on the set members' issues and presentation and their need for support and challenge. The set may help the presenter work through the issues and even make recommendations, but it will not make a decision for the presenter in the way a meeting will. While a set may develop rules relating to timings and produce minutes the minutes are not a record of discussion but the action points agreed – what, when, who, where and how.

Counselling group – while every set member can expect to be listened to, questioned and challenged, they should not expect counselling. A set is not an arena for personal problems, as it focuses on work-related issues and implementation. Furthermore, set members rarely possess the helping skills to deal with personal problems.

Awareness group – while participation in a set will heighten self-awareness, this is a by-product rather than the main benefit or objective.

Self-development group – the emphasis is less on self-discovery than on action and implementation.

Support group – while a set is a valuable source of support to every member and may provide strong group identity, it is also concerned with challenging the individual, often quite assertively, and helping them move on. Responsibility for implementation rests not with the set, but firmly on the shoulders of each participating individual.

Benefits of action learning

For the organization

an organization investing in its people through the provision of action learning programmes will find that it gains more than projects – it will receive an interest on its investment, developed individuals and the development of the organization itself. (McGill and Beaty, 1992)

The focus of action learning projects is the workplace, and in recent years projects have taken an increasingly strategic or cross-functional aspect so that an element of the unfamiliar is present. Organizations that carry out action learning projects and implement them should receive a return on their investment several times over. It is important that in deciding to set up action learning sets the focus is not on the cost, which initially can be viewed as high, but on the return.

Action learning is an excellent way of developing managers while simultaneously solving real-life organizational problems.

As managers learn by doing, the transfer of learning is immediate. Managers learn not only 'what' to do but 'how' to address issues, and the organization builds up a bank of expertise with a multitude of skills, which can then be passed on to other managers.

> Action Learning – developing while simultaneously solving real organisation problems – is the central idea that organisations must embed in their way of life. Action Learning entails putting individuals and teams at risk, role modelling new behaviours, and learning to blend hard business problem solving with soft cultural and behavioural skills. (Tichy, 1994)

Projects can start at any time as and when the need arises. Organizations that have experience in the action learning approach can reduce the start-up time and the time taken to get to implementation.

Action learning will enable organizations to cope with uncertainty and continuous and rapid change. In the present age of flatter structures, reduced hierarchies, generalists rather than specialists, the global village and the information superhighway, the only certainty for organizations is change. People have to learn to adapt and respond accordingly. In order to cope with this change, managers must develop different mind-sets or ways of seeing the world. If they become too entrenched in their thinking they will lack the capacity to adapt and the organization will fail to respond.

The wider the involvement of all layers of management in such projects in a variety of appropriate roles – set members, set adviser, client, expert, mentor – the greater the level of understanding there will be of the process. Such a wide organizational involvement increases project commitment, ownership of solutions and the organization's commitment to training and development. Long term, a training and development culture is established.

The individual

A powerful personal development tool, action learning is based on individuals learning from experience through reflection and action. It utilizes the power of the experiential learning cycle to

Selection of Options

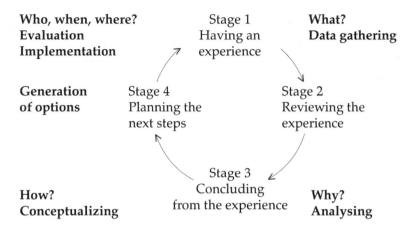

Who, when, where?   Stage 1   **What?**
Evaluation   Having an   **Data gathering**
Implementation   experience

Generation   Stage 4   Stage 2
of options   Planning the   Reviewing the
                    next steps   experience

                        Stage 3
How?   Concluding   **Why?**
Conceptualizing   from the experience **Analysing**

Figure 5.3   *Skill acquisition and the learning cycle*

help managers learn how to learn and as a vehicle for professional and personal development.

The Honey and Mumford learning cycle is given in Figure 5.3; at each stage the main form of questioning and some of the skills that set members will acquire are shown.

In terms of a project, each set member needs to go through the following process:

- collecting data using a variety of methods such as literature search, interviewing, questionnaire design and construction
- analysing the data into meaningful terms
- relating the data to existing theories, concepts and models and possibly formulating new ones
- generating a range of options available
- selecting options and evaluating them
- implementing the preferred option(s).

Each stage of the project requires different skills and expertise, which every set member will not possess to the same degree. Help and support is therefore provided either from other set members or from an expert who may be the set adviser.

The use of the experiential learning cycle helps managers learn how to learn. In Chapter 3 the relationship between the learning cycle and learning styles is given. Understanding your learning preferences and developing the weaker ones produces a more effective learner. Other benefits of action learning for the individual are that: it enables the individual to adopt a positive approach to life. It is the antithesis of believing that we are incapable of doing nothing about a situation. In 1970 NASA was on the receiving end of one of the great understatements of history: 'Houston, we have a problem'. An explosion in the fuel tanks of the service module had put the Apollo 13 spacecraft out of action and nobody knew what to do next. Many 'comrades in adversity' asked the right questions and several days later the crew of Apollo 13 were returned safely to earth.

Another benefit is that, like client-centred counselling, action learning is in tune with the spirit of the age in that it enables managers to learn to accept responsibility for self. Set members will support and help, but will not solve the problem and will certainly not implement the solution. Ownership of the problem and solution through to implementation are several successful steps on the journey to personal empowerment. Continuous learning, which action learning provides, for both knowledge and process skills, is immediately transferable to the workplace and managers feel and see fast results. Among the skills which are developed are:

- giving and receiving feedback
- counselling and mentoring skills
- interpersonal skills
- project team-leading and team-working skills
- problem-solving, planning and goal-setting skills
- oral and written presentation skills.

These are in addition to the skills outlined in Figure 5.3.

Action learning also increases self-awareness. This results from lengthy introspection, from successes and failures and from feedback from others, notably fellow set members and the set adviser. In addition, it offers excellent opportunities to increase a manager's profile within the organization with consequent effects on career progression, and it values and develops the whole person. It acknowledges the existence of feelings as well as thoughts, offers the opportunity for increased self-esteem and enables the individual to proceed towards self-actualization. Action learning enables managers to develop thinking skills and to develop competence at effecting personal change for themselves.

> Now more than ever, organisations and their members face the dual problem of how to do it right and how to do it well. In the process, the whole concept of competence is changing. Whereas in the past, managerial competence went hand in hand with the possession of specific skills and abilities, it now seems to involve much more. Increasingly, it rests in the development of attitudes, values and 'mindset' that allow managers to confront, understand and deal with a wide range of forces within and outside their organisations, as well as in the development of operational skills. (Morgan, 1988)

Types of action learning sets

There are two major types of set, distinguished from each other by sponsorship.

Sets sponsored by the organization

These would include sets formed within an organization to undertake specifically organization-related projects. Sometimes these are part of a major management development programme and linked to obtaining an qualification.

In the late 1980s, and early 1990s, a number of organizations have sponsored in-company action learning MBA programmes; included among these are:

UK	Trafalgar House Construction Holdings Ltd
	Carnaudmetalbox (CMB)
	Allied Irish Bank
	Pilkington Glass
	Dupont
Australia	ICI
South Africa	National Sorghum Breweries

In addition, many organizations have sent managers on open programmes leading to a qualification, either because there were insufficient resources or managers to form an in-company set, or because it was felt the managers sponsored would gain more from the cross-fertilization of ideas and methods to be gained from joining a set composed of a wide cross-section of managers. All organization-sponsored sets need a champion to argue for the release of resources and the more senior the champion, the greater is the likelihood of success. Such champions are usually familiar with the benefits, notably the return on the investment and the power in personal development terms of the action learning process.

Independent action learning sets

These can be found within or across organizations. The organization is not involved in creating the set, determining the boundaries or providing resources. They are formed to meet personal needs. Such sets have a number of advantages:

- they are free from all organizational constraints
- set members can bring issues to set meetings that they could not bring to organization-supported sets
- they can operate open membership so that a wide cross-section of employment groups may be invited to become involved
- their only accountability is to themselves and not the organization.

The major disadvantages are:

- the commitment to the set and its maintenance may make severe demands on the time and resources of each set member. The absence of organizational support may preclude set members from making the required commitment
- the absence of organizational support, especially funding, means that costs have to be borne by the set. The major cost will probably be engaging external expertise, notably a set adviser.

Both sponsored and independent sets can either be facilitated by a set adviser or self-facilitated. In the author's experience, a set adviser is usually required, particularly in the early days of a set's life and especially when an action learning approach is being introduced into an organization for the first time. In the future, in a more unpredictable world which will see a move away from rigid, hierarchical structures to alternative and more flexible forms of working, the need to use self-facilitated sets will probably increase. Developing set adviser skills in the long term within an organization would have much to recommend it. While human resource professionals are the most obvious source, line management are also a potential source of future set advisers.

The role of the set adviser

The set adviser is not a teacher in the traditional sense of imparting knowledge, but a facilitator. Facilitation is defined by Bentley (1994) as:

> the provision of opportunities, resources, encouragement and support for the group to succeed in achieving its objectives and to do this through enabling the group to take control and responsibility for the way they proceed.

There are three main areas of the facilitation process:

- *subject expert* – the set adviser will be expected to make an input of 'P' in their chosen field of expertise
- *process consultant* – this refers to the way in which Set members decide to learn and deal with their content, ie how they operate
- *group management* – every set needs to decide what encouragement and support it will need, how it will proceed, and what demands and involvement it will require from the set adviser. This is a contracting process which will evolve during the life of the set.

Remembering the equation $L = P + Q$, the relationship between P and Q will alter as the set evolves, as shown in Figure 5.4. With the passage of time and the evolution of the set, the amount of input (initially high) from the set adviser will decrease, possibly to zero. The set begins to take increasing

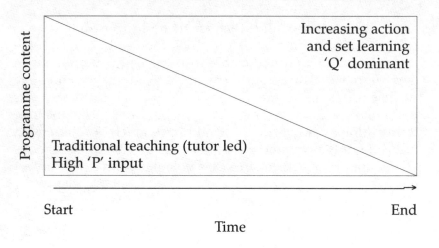

Figure 5.4 *The evolving content of an action learning programme*

responsibility for its own learning so that the role of the set adviser changes from tutor to process consultant. It is a key role of the set adviser to wean the set off its dependency so that it becomes more self-directing.

The set adviser should have the following major goals to be reached by the time the set disbands:

- clearly measurable outputs in terms of work-related projects are completed for presentation to the sponsoring organization which has the option to implement if appropriate;
- set members are empowered to believe in themselves and help themselves in the future, and from this platform of increased self-confidence, can explore and strive to reach their own potential by taking responsibility for their own learning and development;
- increased self-awareness for set members. Casey (1987) suggests that learning about oneself can only be reached through some level of pain and set members are unwilling and unable to push each other through a level of pain. In a set, pain usually comes from challenging and confronting, and this role frequently falls to the set adviser: 'Your pain is the breaking of the shell that encloses your understanding.' (Gibran, 1926).

Operating with sets for chief executives, Casey states,

> in Sets, many participants believe that their ignorance is the shell that encloses their understanding, so they come hoping to dispel some of that ignorance. They see the other Set members as intriguing sources of *knowledge* and they are aware that they themselves are valuable sources of knowledge for the others. And so it turns out to be. They probe each other's experience and knowledge by increasingly skilful questioning. They learn to give and receive. And certainly many shells are broken – but often they are only shells of ignorance.
>
> Participants go away satisfied, with their ignorance reduced. Hard-won knowledge has been traded. But Kahlil Gibran wrote that *pain* is the breaking of the shell of your *understanding*, not your knowledge; these participants have suffered no pain, so their understanding remains where it was when we started. Knowledge can be gained by breaking into shells from the outside, understanding can be gained only by breaking out from your own shell, from the inside.

Some skills of facilitation

Subject expert

Being an 'expert' is most important at the start of the life of the set and to help establish credibility. Therefore at this stage, skills in presenting are needed. As the set evolves this particular skill should be less to the fore as the skill changes to one of recognizing the expertise and knowledge in the set, and harnessing it for the benefit of all.

Group manager

As the set evolves, the responsibility for direction is handed over to the set. The time required for this change will vary and the facilitator should 'let go' at an appropriate rate according to the set's readiness to direct itself. At no stage should facilitation be equated with either control or manipulation.

The key skill that emerges relates to intervention. Knowing when and how to intervene is one that is only developed through experience. Intervening can take numerous forms, each one of them requiring a skill development, and these include:

- challenging the group or its members about outcomes or its way of working
- encouraging when the way ahead is unclear
- 'mirroring back' or summarizing what has been discussed, in an objective and unbiased manner
- giving feedback to individuals, the set, on the way of working, or the outcomes, which may include written assignments
- counselling individuals when problems arise
- asking open and probing questions
- coaching individuals and the set
- knowing when to 'let go', in a way that the set swims and does not sink.

Process consultant

This mainly includes advising and commenting upon how the set operates and deals with its content and learnings.

Characteristics of a good facilitator

Some of the main characteristics are:

- sensitivity to people and situations; this is vitally important if interventions are to be successfully made
- perception and quickness of mind
- tolerance of ambiguity
- patience
- openness, candour and trust; this is important if a trusting and open climate is to be established within the set
- a strong desire to see others learn and develop; they should rejoice in other's success.
- empathy – being capable of 'operating through the mind of another person'
- conceptual ability
- high awareness of self
- recognition of the importance of process as well as content and end product.

Introducing action learning into your organization

Every organization wishing to use action learning will need to decide on its own particular brand and then let it evolve. There is no one prescriptive model. Your intentions may vary from a small, independent action learning set through to implementing a full in-company or consortia management development programme through to qualification. There are, of course, various options in between. Whatever the breadth and scale, a number of recommendations can be made. You should:

- have a number of identified individuals and projects to form an action learning set;
- spend some time preparing and planning; don't rush blindly into it. It is advisable at the start to get good, professional consultancy. A one- or two-day workshop, 'introduction to action learning' for all those to be involved is probably a good idea;
- get involvement and support. You often need a champion, and a senior manager (ideally the chief executive) who is fully sold on the action learning approach will do wonders. In addition, the involvement of senior managers in the various roles of sponsor, client, mentor and presenter is recommended. If a full scale in-company management development programme eventually results, then the involvement of a good cross-section of senior managers in a steering group will pay dividends;
- stay close to the set. This does not mean adopting a 'big brother' approach as that could stifle progress, but they will require regular encouragement and support; and
- look for every opportunity to implement set recommendations. Monitor this and try to establish any quantitative assessment of benefit and, where this can be measured, ensure that key decision makers are fully aware of these benefits.

Good luck! Learn to go with the flow!

Summary

Some of the main points about action learning:

- It is a powerful management and organizational development method that utilizes real managers working on real problems in the organization.
- Managers learn how to learn and it is an appropriate method for all levels in the organization.
- It uses the experience and expertise of the set, and set members learn valuable process skills as well as knowledge.
- Learning is immediately transferable.
- It is a higher risk method than traditional learning, but should repay an organization's investment many times over.
- The role of people providing help for members of the set is essentially and crucially different from that of the normal management teacher. Their role is not to teach but to help managers learn from exposure to problems and to each other.
- The role of the set adviser is crucial, and organizations should build up a pool of suitable people who can apply their facilitation skills to sets.

References and further reading

Bentley, T (1994) *Facilitation, providing opportunities for learning*, Maidenhead: McGraw-Hill.

Casey, D (1976) 'The emerging role of the set adviser in action learning programmes', *Journal of European Training*, 5, 3.

Casey, D (1987) 'Breaking the shell that encloses your understanding', *Journal of Management Development*, 6 No. 2.

Gibran, Kahlil (1926) *The Prophet*, London: Heinemann.

Inglis, S (1994) *Making the Most of Action Learning*, Aldershot: Gower.

McGill, I and Beaty, L (1992) *Action Learning: A practitioner's guide*, London: Kogan Page.

Margerison, C (1989) *Action Learning. A short managerial guide*, Bradford: MCB University Press.

Morgan, G (1988) *Riding the Waves of Change*, San Francisco, CA:

Jossey Bass.

Mumford, A (1984) (ed) *Insights in Action Learning*, Bradford: MCB University Press.

Pedler, M (1991) *Action Learning in Practice*, (2nd edn), Aldershot: Gower.

Revans, R W (1971) *Developing Effective Managers*, London: Longman.

Revans, R W (1982) *The Origins and Growth of Action Learning*, Bromley: Chartwell Bratt.

Revans, R W (1983) *The ABC of Action Learning*, Bromley: Chartwell Bratt.

Tichy, Noel (1994) in 'The Future of Workplace Learning and Performance' in *The Past, Present and Future of Workplace Learning*, Alexandria, VA: ASTD.

Chapter 6

Mentoring

He that hath the steerage of my course
Direct my sail.

(Romeo and Juliet, Act 1, Scene 4)

What is mentoring?

The word 'mentor' is derived from Greek mythology. Ulysses, prior to setting out on one of his epic voyages, left his son, Telemactus, to the custody and tutelage of his old friend, Mentor. The adoption of the term from the name has since been applied to a situation in which an older, wiser and more experienced person offers a young, or less experienced, person the benefits of their help, guidance and patronage.

The mentoring process was most obvious in the old apprenticeship system in which the young were paired with a master craftsman who would gradually pass on his know-how over the years. In the USA, mentoring has been used widely since the 1960s as a way of developing high-potential managers and assisting career development. An article in the *Harvard Business Review* (1979) by Gerald Roche who surveyed over 1,200 executives showed that over two-thirds had benefited from mentorship at one stage in their careers and were happy with their career progression.

Definitions of mentoring vary but a number were assembled by Audrey Collin in an article in the *Industrial and Commercial Training* journal (1988) and included the following:

a mentor is an influential person who significantly helps you reach your life goals mentoring is a process in which one person (mentor) is responsible for overseeing the career and development of another person (protégé) outside the normal manager/subordinate relationship.

mentoring is a protected relationship in which learning and experimentation can occur, potential skills can be developed and in which results can be increased in terms of competencies gained rather than curricular territory covered.

This last definition suggests that there could be greater scope for the use of mentoring in the UK in the decade ahead, as management or business qualifications become more work-related or competency-based and move away from the traditional acquisition of knowledge acquired in traditional academic institutions.

As the world of work undergoes significant change, as our understanding of the adult learning process deepens, and as we increasingly recognize the number of development or learning opportunities that exist outside the formal confines of a training course, the attractions of mentorship as one of a number of ways in which organizations can develop their people become more obvious. Some situations in which mentorship could be the appropriate developmental vehicle are:

- On graduate induction programmes to cover a graduate's early days in the organization. Pilkington Glass introduced such a scheme in the mid-1980s in an attempt to minimize wastage.
- Assisting young professionals gain further qualifications. Examples of this are an articled clerk in a legal practice who is seeking a qualification, or a teacher, either in his or her probationary year or a mid-career teacher pursuing a course of post-graduate study while in post.
- The development of high potential ('Hi-Po') managers to be the senior managers of the future. Many organizations, recognizing the scarcity of good managerial talent and the cost of recruiting externally, have chosen to develop home-grown talent through elaborate management development programmes. Trafalgar House Construction Holdings operated a four-year MBA programme by action learning for middle managers from 1988, for which the author was set

adviser for four sets. A mentorship programme for course associates ran in tandem with the course.

- In assisting the induction and development of people who were previously recognized as 'disadvantaged' as they return to work. In the UK the impact of equal opportunities legislation has manifested itself in greater employment opportunities for women, ethnic minorities, physically and mentally handicapped individuals and so on. In some of these instances, support on its own is of great value, irrespective of the benefits of tutelage.
- A new recruit in a work situation of continued change may require an element of stability in order to keep a sense of perspective. Neville Cheadle (1987) of the consultancy firm Price Waterhouse said,

A new joiner will find our matrix structure quite complex ... one goes to a particular project, builds up a relationship and then the team is disbanded and one starts another project with another manager. So what we do to provide some sort of continuity and help is to appoint a mentor manager for the new joiner and he will help him find his way around, identify interesting and challenging assignments and really just introduce him into the firm.

- To a manager given an overseas posting which will involve some adaptation to new working methods and styles, family adjustments and particularly adapting to a new culture in which what may have been the norm in the home country is taboo in the adopted country. A mentor can be a valuable source of both information and support in the adjustment and adaptation process.

This brief introduction to mentoring suggests that there is no one overall definition, and also that there is no one type of organization or situation in which it should apply. The degree of formality relating to the scheme will also vary considerably. Support and development are two key aspects of the mentoring process and these are at the very core of the mentoring philosophy. The design and operations of the mentoring scheme must therefore be tailored appropriately to the needs of the individual and the organization.

Benefits of mentoring

Mentoring can be made to work in most organizations over the long term, given the commitment. With proper planning it can be an extremely cost-effective way of developing talent and increasing staff awareness of all that takes place within the organization. Mentoring does not require a number of expensive off-site courses, although an initial course at the start of the programme should be offered. Once up and running the programme operates on site. Two surveys in the late 1980s studied mentoring both internationally and within the UK. The PA International Survey (1987) listed the most common benefits to companies as follows:

- improved succession planning and management development
- faster induction of new employees
- better communications
- reduced training costs
- increased productivity
- reduced labour costs.

The Industrial Society/ITEM Group survey of British companies (1990) found the main reasons for introducing a mentoring scheme into UK companies were:

- to support a self-development programme
- faster induction
- increased retention of staff
- better identification of potential
- ensuring professional qualifications are maintained
- development for the mentor
- building relationships.

Some of these benefits will now be discussed in more detail, although not necessarily in order of importance.

Better induction of new employees and socialization into the organization

All new employees, whatever their level of competence, have to ascend a learning curve when taking up a post, whether it be developing technical expertise, managerial competence or tuning-in to the norms and values of the organization. Most staff turnover occurs during the first six months as the new incumbent comes to terms with the new environment. Any support system will help reduce the period of adjustment and socialization into the new environment, which in the case of newly recruited graduates, fresh from university, can be almost traumatic.

A mentoring programme as part of a management development programme can also assist an organization's recruitment drive. It transmits a caring image in which the employee is valued as a person and shows that the organization is committed to staff retention and development. 'There are career prospects with us and we will help you' is the message.

Improved communications

Learning the organization's communication network, both formal and informal, takes time. It is usually learnt on the job rather than on a formal course. A mentor, along with the line manager, can be a valuable tutor in helping the protégé learn about the existence of, and how to use, these networks. Improved communications can, in the long run, only improve individual productivity and organizational efficiency.

Reduced training costs

Off-site management training programmes are expensive. A mentoring programme requires only a little (although vitally important) training of mentors before the programme commences. Mentors will learn more through experience than by formal instruction which needs to be recorded as the programme develops.

Inevitably some managers will take to mentoring better than others. The experience and expertise of these managers needs to be tapped and utilized for subsequent training on second and third wave programmes, so that the cost of initial training is considerably reduced.

Increased motivation and productivity

Mentoring can help reduce staff turnover for both mentor and protégé. New, young employees, particularly if they are graduates, often have unrealistic career expectations. They expect a rapid rise up the company career ladder and such expectations may not be met. This is even more likely with the current trend towards flatter organizations with fewer rungs in the organization ladder. A mentor can help the protégé look for ways around the current blockages and reinforce the message from the company that there is a future for him or her. The result could be that other organizations do not poach your employees by promising fast career advancement.

The trend to flatter organizations has posed career problems for middle and senior managers who also will have fewer rungs to ascend up the corporate ladder. The effect of this is that 'plateau-ing' can occur earlier. Being too long in a job can result in mental retirement and reduced motivation as few new challenges arise. A mentoring relationship can provide a fresh challenge, reduce boredom and perhaps make the mentor improve his or her own performance in order to gain and maintain the respect of the protégé. A bright young graduate on the doorstep can have a stimulating and energising effect on the mentor. The flame of interest and commitment which was facing extinction may be rekindled.

Better succession planning and management development

Mentoring is a cost-effective way of developing managers and should be used along with other methods. It is an important part of the whole picture. Participation in a scheme should lead to a considerable increase in interpersonal skills and a valuable extra input from the mentor into succession planning. Mentors may also help identify potential which a line manager cannot, or will not, see.

Transfer of knowledge and values of the organization and maintenance of a more stable corporate culture

Mentors can become powerful role models for protégés and the latter can learn much by imitation and identification with the mentor. The protégé will observe methods, styles and how things are done, becoming more acutely aware of the managerial style of the organization and this, if internalized and translated into action, will ensure a less painful adjustment if he or she is promoted. The smooth transfer of company culture between two generations of managers can provide both stability and change and assist long-term corporate growth and survival.

Benefits to the protégé

The PA International Survey listed the most common benefits for protégés as follows:

- personal support
- teaching and counselling
- career planning
- knowledge and awareness of the company
- role modelling
- commitment to the company.

Some of these benefits will now be discussed in more detail, although not necessarily in order of importance.

Personal support and induction for those coming from higher education and those taking an overseas posting

Moving from the world of higher education to the world of work is one of the major changes in our lives. For some it can cause a major shock to the system! What is expected from us changes beyond recognition and the new expectations have to be learned quickly. Similarly, those of us who have had to cope with the culture shock of an overseas posting have experienced trepidations. The assignment of a mentor in these early stages of adjustment can be invaluable in providing a support service as well as speedy, informal tuition on the 'dos' and 'don'ts' of our new world.

Career advice and advancement

Mentors can be invaluable for career advice and counselling. They can be a role model and demonstrate that certain behaviours can bring their just reward. They can explain how organizations are structured and how they function, and they can offer advice on possible career moves and what experience should be acquired in order to make that move. If the worst comes to the worst and the protégé is made redundant, a well-respected mentor can be a source of emotional support, offering sound advice on the job search and possibly finding an opening through his or her network of contacts outside the organization. There is nothing to beat a personal recommendation to get a foot in the door.

A mentor can also help to raise the protégé's profile in the organization by involving him or her on the mentor's own projects, taking the protégé to his or her own meetings and possibly asking the protégé to present to an audience. With good briefing and evaluation the protégé can gain a good insight into how groups function, how meetings are conducted and how decisions are reached. Mentors can open doors and gain protégés the kind of exposure that would be denied them if they paddled their own canoe.

Such support and mentoring should improve the protégé's self-confidence. Confidence breeds competence and competence should mean greater personal effectiveness. The very fact that the protégé has been assigned a mentor tells the protégé that the organization values him or her as an individual. Additionally, a mentor should be a source of valuable feedback on performance, and positive feedback is a great confidence booster.

Learning to cope with the formal and informal structure of the organization

Every organization has its formal and informal aspect, its overt and covert ways of getting things done. Through a mentor the protégé should learn about the overt ways – procedures, communication channels and networks, culture, values, etc – and its covert ways such as internal company politics, influencing of key decision makers and where best and with whom to be seen.

Managerial tutelage

As a role model, and possibly as a tutor, the mentor can be an excellent source of tuition for the protégé. It may also sharply contrast with earlier tuition in management. A protégé fresh from university or business school may find tuition from a manager reared in the 'school of hard knocks' or the 'university of life' provides a different perspective and more practical advice.

The mentor may also be a sounding board for problems/issues in the protégé's work area. As the mentor is usually external to the protégé work area, counselling or advice given will normally be free of any bias and also offer an alternative and experienced insight into a situation from which the mentor is distanced, so increasing the likelihood of objectivity and at the same time offering advice that would be in the protégé's best interests. In short, work is integrated with self-development for the benefit of all.

It may also arise that the protégé wishes to confide in his or her mentor a personal problem. At most a sympathetic hearing can help the protégé unload his or her problems; at best the mentor may have the appropriate counselling skills or suggest help with getting specialist assistance.

Skills of tutoring and counselling are high on the list of the competences a mentor needs and separate chapters have been devoted to these in this book.

Benefits to the mentor

The PA and Industrial Society/ITEM surveys listed the following as the main benefits:

- job enrichment
- psychic rewards such as pride and a feeling of self-awareness
- better organizational communication
- career advancement.

Job enrichment

Like parenting, developing a young employee can be a challenging and rewarding experience. There is a sense of pride and achievement when the protégé does well. As organizations develop flatter structures, career paths are less clearly defined and mentoring can provide a fresh challenge and enrich the job. In extreme cases a 'plateau-ed' manager may even take greater satisfaction from their protégé's achievement than their own.

Mentoring can also be a great learning process. As any teacher will tell you, teaching a subject or individual is an excellent way to learn or update. Additionally, mentors who are graduates of the 'university of life' have the opportunity to learn from the graduate from the university or business school. Learning from others is another excellent way of gaining new information and fresh insights, and it is never too late to learn.

Increased self-awareness

The process of helping others gain knowledge and skills can be a powerful way of reflecting on one's own strengths and weaknesses. Self-awareness is a lifelong process and new opportunities and new roles teach us much about ourselves.

Better organizational communication

Protégés are a great source of information, providing useful 'bottom-up' feedback on organizational activities. Mentors can therefore be a general agent in improving organization communication. Additionally, regular contact with those lower down the organization gives the mentor feedback from a different perspective and helps the mentor stay in touch with views from the grass roots.

Career advancement

Mentorship is increasingly seen as a core management skill essential to all managers. Mentors can help their promotion prospects by delegating work to previously mentored managers, and thereby also increase their own efficiency. The choice of delegate is always crucial, but having insight into the person from a previous mentoring relationship should give the manager a thorough insight into strengths and ways of working. The chances of making the right choice of who to delegate what task to should be greater.

Protégés can also assist career development by possibly being groomed as the mentor's successor, or by being a useful contact if the protégé rises to a higher position later in life.

Finally, recognition from peers or superiors of the mentor as one who develops high potential employees can only enhance the reputation of the mentor in the eyes of senior management.

Potential problems of mentoring

Mentoring should not be seen as the only form of human resource development in an organization, but as an addition to already existing programmes. Nevertheless, it can achieve some powerful and positive effects, given that the culture is right for the process and that the process is carefully monitored and evaluated. Many companies which have operated mentoring programmes have claimed success and many positive benefits, and some of these have been described. Nevertheless, problems do occur and awareness of these beforehand can produce a proactive response from the training department so that they are either 'nipped in the bud' or their negative effects are minimized.

The PA survey and the survey by the Industrial Society/ ITEM group revealed the following as the main problems associated with mentoring:

- inadequate definition of mentor–protégé role
- communication difficulties between mentor and protégé, especially the inability to give negative feedback constructively
- lack of commitment
- resentment from protégé's line manager
- poor selection and pairing of mentor and protégé.

These can be discussed under the following four broad headings.

Problems with selection

Selection for anything usually involves an element of rejection. Not everyone is suitable, or rejection may be purely on the grounds of lack of available places. Rejected candidates may feel disappointed and resentful and these people can cause harm in the organization. Allegations of favouritism or feelings of inadequacy can surface among rejected candidates, while envy and resentment from a protégé's peers who may perceive the successful protégé as a 'crown prince' can often hinder a mentoring relationship. It is therefore important that organizations:

- ensure that everyone knows the criteria for selection and that those criteria are applied as fairly as possible
- ensure that those not selected for a mentoring scheme are informed as sensitively and empathetically as possible
- stress in the feedback to unsuccessful candidates that mentoring is only one of many routes to career development.
- consider the reactions of unsuccessful candidates and take steps to minimize any adverse effects these may have.

Relationship difficulties

In the same way that all marriages are not successful, so mentoring relationships can fail. Among the reasons this may happen are:

- The two parties are mismatched and never achieve the degree of openness and trust required.
- All relationships need an investment of time and energy which hectic work schedules do not permit.
- Unreasonable expectations from either mentor or protégé. The mentor may be too controlling, restricting the protégé's individuality and inclination to 'give it a go'. As sometimes happens with a line relationship, the protégé is held back in the fear that the protégé will outgrow the relationship and could outstrip the mentor in the future. Alternatively, protégés may expect that mentors will transform their careers overnight and when this fails to happen feel resentful and betrayed and may walk away from the relationship.
- Mentors may withdraw support if they feel that imminent failure by the protégé in a highly visible role will undermine their own credibility in the eyes of others. The same applies in reverse. Neither party may want to be seen to attach themselves to a falling star.
- Failure to keep boundaries between professional and personal friendship issues; if something goes wrong in the latter it can impact on the former.
- In the case of cross-gender mentoring the importance of boundary-keeping is even greater. The effects of gossip and sexual innuendos can be extremely damaging, whether true or false.

Power/role conflicts

'Two's company, three's a crowd' is an old cliché but in any threesome one party usually feels excluded. If the line manager is the excluded party, problems and power conflicts can arise. Feelings of jealousy and resentment can also creep in if the line manager perceives the protégé as being groomed for advancement, so that in years ahead the present pecking order will be reversed. Problems can also occur if those in the mentor/ protégé relationship throughout the organization are seen to form an exclusive club open only to the few. Line managers may wonder about what goes on at such meetings and whether their own position is being undermined.

Working priorities

The protégé may become more concerned with pleasing his or her mentor at the expense of their manager so that job-related tasks may suffer. Again, resentment and opposition from the protégé's line manager may occur.

Steps to implementing a mentoring programme

Earlier in the book (see Figure 1.3) the training triangle was discussed in relation to training needs. In mentoring, the triangle becomes a quadrangle, consisting of:

- the mentor
- the protégé
- the line manager
- the trainer/training department, who monitor the programme and provide training opportunities to meet needs.

In addition a fifth party is involved – senior management – whose support and commitment is vital. The various parties are shown in Figure 6.1.

Preceding chapters and previous discussions in this chapter should have highlighted a number of prerequisites for the implementation of a mentoring programme in the organization; these would include the following:

- A culture in which learning is a key and valued feature and in which informal and formal development opportunities are encouraged.

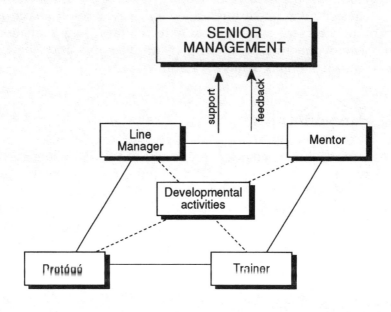

Figure 6.1 *Mentoring relationships*

- Top management are seen to be committed and supportive. Their presence at all stages of the scheme will do much to raise enthusiasm and maintain motivation and commitment.
- Participants, both mentors and protégés, are volunteers, not conscripts and selection criteria are well-defined. There is more chance of success if mentor and protégé select each other rather than having a relationship imposed on them: arranged marriages can cause resentment.
- Mentors should be properly briefed as to what is involved and trained in the skills required. Training in counselling, coaching and training skills are among the most important. The training should be seen as ongoing so that not only is a pool of mentors built up, but a support network exists from either fellow mentors, the training department or line managers. Mentors should have the opportunity to meet at regular intervals to share and compare experiences and advise each other on the challenges they face.
- The scheme is monitored and evaluated regularly; and the training department should play a key role in this process.

- Drawing up clear terms of reference for all parties. They should include guidelines on confidentiality, views, timetable of meetings (if any) between mentor and protégé, support services for mentors if relationship difficulties arise, and so on.
- A realistic time-frame is set up. Each section of the programme should be short, about 6–12 months.
- The programme should be part of a wider, management development programme.
- The scheme should be communicated widely so the whole organization is aware of it and everyone knows what they should know.

As a starting point, the checklist on pages 112–13 in question format should help in the implementation of a mentoring scheme. Space has been left in each section for you to make the occasional short note.

Summary

Some of the major points in this chapter.

- From early origins, mentoring has been increasingly seen as a valuable and cost-effective management development tool and a powerful career development vehicle. There are many situations which can arise in organizational life for which mentoring could be an appropriate solution.
- Mentoring can bring many benefits for individuals, notably:
  - better induction
  - career advice and advancement
  - improved self-confidence and self-awareness
  - job enrichment
  - improved communication skills.
- Mentoring can bring many benefits to organizations, notably:
  - more rapid induction and socialization into the organization
  - preservation of a stable corporate culture
  - improved communications
  - reduced training costs

CHECKLIST

1. **Culture**

   Is the culture or climate right for a scheme in this organization?

   Is there anything I can do to create a more favourable climate?

2. **Top management support**

   Will top management be committed to the scheme?

   How should they be approached?

   How should this best be displayed?

   How should I best get them involved?

3. **Objectives**

   What are my objectives?

   What is a realistic time-frame?

4. **Resources**

   What financial resources will I need and what will the break-down be?

   Who will need to be involved and where?

5. **Selection**

   How will I select mentors?

   How will I select protégés?

6. **Training**

   How will I train mentors?

   Who will train them?

   What needs to be included in the training programme?

7. **Terms of reference and guidelines**

   What do these need to include?

   Have I clearly established these and communicated them to all parties?

   What provision must I make for continual updating and modification?

8. **Support systems**

   How can mentors best be supported?

   Who shall I involve?

   What will be needed if problems occur in a mentoring relationship?

9. **Evaluation**

   How shall I evaluate the programme?

   When shall I evaluate the programme?

   Who shall I involve in the evaluation process?

10. **Future developments**

    How can we best share and record experiences and learn from them for the benefit of all?

- better succession planning and wider-management development
- increased motivation and productivity.
- Mentoring programmes can develop numerous problems which careful planning and quality training can reduce.
- Implementation of a mentoring scheme needs careful planning and the active involvement of senior management, line management and training personnel.
- All schemes should be carefully monitored and evaluated and what is learned applied to future schemes.

References and further reading

British Institute of Management (1984) *Creating a Committed Workforce, Proceedings of the Second National Conference,* London: BIM, pp. 5–6.

British Institute of Management (1987) *Mentoring,* MINT Series, 2, 5. London: British Institute of Management.

Carter, S (1994) *An Essential Guide to Mentoring,* Corby: The Institute of Management Foundation.

Cheadle, Neville (1987) quoted in 'The Personal Touch in Management Development', Kate Runciman and Catherine Smith, in *Management Information Notes and Topics (MINT) Series,* Vol 2, No 5. London: British Institute of Management.

Clutterbuck, D (1991) *Everyone Needs a Mentor: Fostering talent at work,* (2nd edn), London: Institute of Personnel Management PA.

Collin, A (1988) 'Mentoring', *Industrial and Commercial Training,* March/April. Bradford: MCB University Press.

Industrial Society and the ITEM Group (1990) *The Line Manager's Role in Developing Talent,* Birmingham: Industrial Society.

Kram, K G (1985) *Mentoring at Work: Developmental relationships in organisational life,* London: Scott Foresman.

PA Personnel Services (1987) *Management Development and Mentoring: An international study,* London: PA.

Phillips Jones, L (1982) *Mentors and Protégés: How to establish, strengthen and get the most from a mentor/protégé relationship,* New York: Arbor House.

Roche, G G (1979) 'Much ado about mentors', *Harvard Business Review,* Jan–Feb.

Zey, M G (1984) *The Mentor Connection,* Illinois: Dow Jones Irwin.

Chapter 7

Self-development

There's only one corner of the Universe you can be certain of improving, and that's your own self. (Aldous Huxley)

As we approach a new millennium, self-development is an increasingly recognized field and more and more individuals are preferring to take responsibility for their own development rather than leave it to others. This is a change of emphasis from years ago when it was widely felt that the responsibility lay with the employing organization. That is not to say that the organization does not provide the means, the support and the arena for such development, but rather that the focus for the initial impetus has changed.

What is self-development?

Self-development must inevitably involve learning and the development of learning abilities or habits. In 1988 Pedler *et al.* described it as:

> an effective system for development which increases the learner's capacity and willingness to take control over and responsibility for, events and particularly for themselves and their own learning.

Self-development as a broad term can be subdivided into three major areas.

1. *Management self-development* – is about how you develop the knowledge, skills and attitudes (nowadays often summa-

rized as 'competences') to make you a more effective manager.

2. *Personal development* – relates to your own desires and
    wishes and how these can be satisfied.

3. *Career development* – relates to the progress you make over a
    period of time within organizations to satisfy your develop-
    ing aspirations.

Inevitably there is a considerable overlap between all three.
Your personal development will be reflected in your performance as a manager and your performance as a manager will be
reflected in your career progress. Also, your life away from
work will offer personal development opportunities that can either be savoured as opportunities in their own right or transferred to the work place to improve managerial effectiveness.
Furthermore, with a move towards flatter structures, opportunities for career advancement in terms of hierarchical progression
are being considerably reduced, so many individuals will seek
personal development opportunities to satisfy needs that the
organization can no longer meet. This chapter will focus on all
three forms of self-development and suggest a number of ways
in which individuals can satisfy their development needs.

Why encourage self-development?

A number of arguments can be advanced.

*   Individuals have an inherent desire to learn new skills and
    knowledge. In the past traditional training has not provided
    the means to satisfy this desire, nor did it offer the flexibility
    required. Many self-development activities, such as open
    learning, can be pursued at times to suit the learner's con-
    venience.
*   To continue the trend in training and development of mov-
    ing the focus away from the trainer to the learner. The
    wealth of research that has taken place in the field of adult
    learning in the last 30 years has confirmed that the adult
    learner dislikes being taught, but enjoys learning, especially
    when it is relevant to their own reality, is participative and
    gives a rapid return on endeavours. Consequently, many

training and development activities are learner- and experientially-focused. Furthermore, each individual has a preferred style of learning and can now choose the most appropriate way to learn.

- Newly acquired knowledge and skills usually enable individuals to improve their job performance. The majority of people want to do their job to the best of their abilities.
- To develop people's careers either within the present organization or elsewhere. With flatter structures and down-sizing, employing organization may not offer the prospects desired, so individuals will look elsewhere. In other words, they will develop their career across organizations instead of within one organization.
- Individuals have a strong, intrinsic desire to make the best of their potential or to self-actualize. Nowhere is this more evident than among the generation born in the 1960s, dubbed 'generation X' by Douglas Coupland. This new generation frequently views personal development as more important than money, power or even comfort at work.
- As a way of coping with change. It is important not only to increase our knowledge and skill base to cope with the demands of ever-increasing change, but to learn how to learn in order to change ourselves accordingly. People must also become less entrenched in their thinking – if their mind-sets are too rigid and inflexible they may not be able to change and adapt.
- More and more managers are taking on the role of 'developer'. This was endorsed by the 'Developing the Developers Report' (Megginson and Pedler, 1991) published in the UK in which the respondents saw important differences between training and development and they wanted to keep the terms separate. Two-thirds of the 633 respondents in the survey saw themselves more as developers than trainers.

You can hardly develop others if you are not developing yourself; if you are involved in some of the activities outlined in this book – coaching, counselling, mentoring, training, along with some of the areas outlined later in this chapter – you cannot fail to develop in some way. Megginson and Pedler (1992) state that the developers' task in self-development is 'to empower people to learn from acting and to act on the basis of learning'. They believe that the developers' field of work is in four main areas which they refer to as the developers' diamond field, which is shown in Figure 7.1.

Most developers work with individuals and groups but may neglect themselves. Developing yourself is an important prerequisite for effective working with others and for working with, and contributing to, the organization as a whole.

• The establishment of a culture in which learning and development are valued is important to organizational success and the organization's ability to cope with change. Much has been written about the concept of a learning organization, but any organization that creates learning opportunities for its members must transform itself and create a learning culture. Organizations that have people who wait to be taught, cannot act on their own initiative and will refrain from any risk taking, will lack the flexibility and adaptability to change. This is particularly important with medium and smaller-sized organizations who are more at the mercy of the winds of external change than in a position to influence them.

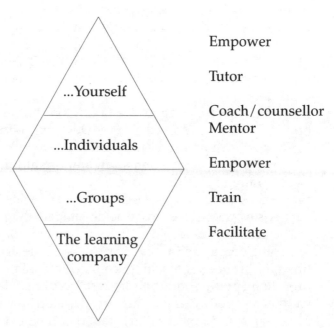

...Yourself	Empower
	Tutor
	Coach/counsellor
	Mentor
...Individuals	Empower
...Groups	Train
The learning company	Facilitate

Figure 7.1 *The developers' diamond field. Adapted from* Self-Development: A Facilitator's Guide, *D Megginson and M Pedler,* © McGraw-Hill *1992, with permission*

Management self-development

All self-development starts with self. It involves empowering oneself to assess one's strengths and weaknesses, drawing up an action plan and seeking out the training and development activities required. For some, the first part in particular may be a painful process (confronting self is never easy) and a firm commitment is required to set and particularly achieve the goals that are set.

Francis and Woodcock (*The Unblocked Manager*, 1982) introduced the blockage concept to help individuals assess their personal development needs and establish a self-development programme. They define a blockage as 'a factor that inhibits the potential output of a system, i.e. the total organisation, team or individual'. If a part of the whole is dysfunctional or blocked, the whole under-performs. At the individual level a blockage is an area of undeveloped competence. In order to bring about rapid self-development, managers must explore, understand and remove blockages that prevent success and personal growth.

Francis and Woodcock identified 11 blockages to effective management, although each blockage will not be equally relevant to every managerial job. The blockages are briefly described below; please note that the opposite of the stated blockage is the competence that managers should be seeking. The identified blockages are:

- *Self-management incompetence* – relates to the effective use of time, energy and skills.
- *Unclear personal values* – managers need clear values to form a sound basis for judgement. In the modern business world, these values must be consistent with managerial effectiveness, developing others to achieve their potential and being open and receptive to innovation.
- *Confused personal goals* – managers who are unclear about their personal and professional goals will not be able to reach their own potential and be less likely to help others in their endeavours.
- *Stunted personal development* – relates to a manager's personal development and willingness to confront weaknesses and work towards personal growth. Managers displaying this blockage are unwilling to risk themselves or accept

challenges and settle for the security of routine and predictability.

- *Inadequate problem-solving skills* – managers in today's world
  need to be skilled at resolving problems and reaching solutions either on their own or in groups.
- *Low creativity* – many managers are left-brain thinkers who
  are unwilling to experiment, take risks or generate creative
  thinking in others. Problems in the global village of the
  present require fast and innovative ideas and solutions.
- *Low influence* – refers to an inability to influence others in
  the organization over whom they have no direct authority.
  Such people are characterized by poor interpersonal skills,
  poor presentation and listening skills and a low level of as-
  sertiveness.
- *Lack of managerial insight* – refers to a lack of understanding
  of human beings, themselves and others. Such people seek
  little feedback from others and are unwilling and unable to
  change their management style.
- *Poor supervisory skills* – refers to an inability to coordinate
  and direct the work of others, causing time and effort to be
  wasted, and is characterized by negative, unproductive relationships.
- *Low trainer capacity* – many managers are now taking on a
  training role. This is necessary to help subordinates develop
  job competence and continue to develop. Managers displaying poor training skills lack the ability to diagnose learning
  needs and to provide effective constructive and appropriate
  support in such areas as counselling and coaching.
- *Low team-building capacity* – refers to a manager's inability to
  achieve results through the collective efforts of the team.
  They lack the required process skills.

The blockage concept is one of several frameworks that offer
managers an opportunity to assess current capability and develop an action plan to develop personal and professional competence. It offers an audit of current needs based on both
self-perception and feedback from others, which should therefore achieve a more accurate and objective assessment of needs.

The removal of some of these blockages can be achieved by a
multitude of methods, some of which are outlined in the next
section.

Personal development

The development of self for personal reasons cannot fail (given a reasonable level of motivation) to impact positively on an individual's performance as a manager. Organizations should therefore encourage individuals to invest in themselves as they should reap the benefits several times over. Furthermore, while an individual may embark on a path of development that may not appear immediately relevant to the needs of the organization, it should be stated that the workplace is changing so rapidly that what is irrelevant now may not be irrelevant in the near future. The development of any new skills should be encouraged as they could be called upon at any time. Short-termism will not achieve much, and if it is really the case that 'our people are our most valuable resource', then action and support, not words, are needed. A number of personal development methods or areas will now be outlined; the list is by no means exhaustive.

Learning to learn

People can only develop if they have learned how to learn. They need to be equipped with the strategies and range of learning styles which are appropriate not only for present learning but which are transferable for the future. Individuals must recognize that opportunities for learning are all around them and the experience needs to be fully utilized and processed.

Learning is not a static or one-off event. It is a continuous process and we need to know what to do, how to do it and when to act, and part of that process is adapting new strategies and strengthening existing styles, however weak. Learning to learn, therefore, is at the very heart of self-development. Two definitions of 'learning to learn' will help clarify the concept further. Mumford (1986) defines the four major elements as:

- helping managers to know the stages of the learning process and blockages to learning;
- helping them understand their own preferred approaches to learning;
- assisting individuals in making the best use of their existing

learning preference, or building additional strengths and overcoming blockages; and
- helping individuals to carry their understanding of learning from off-the-job to on-the-job opportunities.

Smith (1983) defines learning to learn as: 'possessing or acquiring the knowledge and skills to learn effectively in whatever learning situation one encounters'. However, he does stress that there is probably no such thing as a 'complete learner', eg, someone may be effective when learning independently, yet be ineffective in the classroom.

Opportunities for learning are probably greater now than ever. Everyday experience in the workplace, home, in our own time, etc., along with the opportunities provided by new technology, offer rich and varied learning opportunities and what is learned can often be transferable to another area.

Learning logs

A very cost-effective way of learning from everyday experience is to keep a learning log for recording and processing events. Keeping a learning log requires considerable self-discipline and therefore individuals may decide beforehand to contract with themselves to do it for a certain period of time, eg, the duration of a course, secondment, or job exchange. Keeping a learning log requires you to write:

- an account of what happened during an experience, eg, 'I presented my proposals to the meeting and they were rejected';
- a list of the conclusions you have drawn from the experience or event, eg, 'I should have found out beforehand who the key decision makers were', 'I should have canvassed opinions and support beforehand', 'I should have used good visual aids to add impact to my proposals'; and
- a plan of action stating exactly what you are going to do in the light of your conclusions.

There are a number of occasions on which entries can be made, for example:

- during or immediately after a significant event, experience, meeting
- at the end of a significant period of time, eg, a course, a fort-night
- at significant juncture of a major task or project
- at the completion of major tasks or projects.

You may learn in terms of both *content* and *process*. While a learning log is written specifically for yourself, you may find it helpful to review aspects of your log with a colleague, to review your experiences, what you have learned and how you have learned it. The degree to which you may wish to involve others will depend upon whether you wish to risk yourself, but the process of sharing can be very beneficial. People with whom you may want to share could be your mentor, coach, counsellor or fellow member of an action learning set. Keeping and possibly sharing a learning log enables individuals to process an experience and to learn how to learn.

Developing self-awareness

He who knows much about others may be learned, but he who understands himself is more intelligent. He who controls others may be powerful, but he who has mastered himself is mightier still. (Lao Tzu)

Self-awareness underpins all self-development. The mechanism for self-awareness is feedback and that usually comes from two major sources – from psychometric instruments and from others, ie, non-instrumental feedback. Increasing self-awareness involves an element of risk as we may receive messages that make us feel uncomfortable and are sometimes difficult to accept. Great care needs to be given to choosing the appropriate method. The expertise and the interpersonal skills of the person giving feedback is of even greater importance. A number of useful instruments that can aid self-awareness are described below.

Learning Styles Questionnaire (LSQ)

This will give feedback on your preferred learning style. There are four styles – activist, reflector, theorist and pragmatist – and each one corresponds to each of the major stages in the learning cycle. Awareness of preferred and weaker styles can very much assist an individual to learn how to learn.

Personality Questionnaires

These give a profile of certain dimensions of personality. The better tests are both valid and reliable and are administered by a registered test user. Raw scores are usually computed to give a score against a norm bank for different occupational groups. Feedback needs to be considered on this basis and related to the reality of the person completing the test. The person giving feedback needs to obtain clarification of the situation that the person tested had in mind when completing the test, since responses can be situational and therefore variable. The majority of these tests are self-report instruments but a few can be completed by others, eg, one's manager, so that the accuracy of one's own perception can be validated. Among the tests in this category are:

Myers Briggs Type Inventory (MBTI)
Catells 16 Personality Factor (16PF)
SHL Occupational Personality Questionnaire (OPQ)
Gordon's Personal Profile Inventory (GPP–I)
Minnesota Multiphasic Personality Inventory (MMPI)
California Personality Inventory (CPI).

The test selected should be appropriate to the identified need.

Team Role Models

These give feedback to individuals based upon their preferred roles in a team situation. They can be used in team-building exercises and in action learning sets. Among the tests that can be used in this category are:

Belbin Team Role Model
Margerison-McCann Team Management Index (TMI).

Again, the test should be appropriate to the need.

Developing the right brain

> The concept of creativeness and the concept of the healthy, self-actualising, fully human person seem to be coming closer and closer together, and may perhaps turn out to be the same thing. (Maslow, 1968)

The work of Roger Sperry and Robert Ornstein in California in the late 1960s and early 1970s revealed that the brain has two distinct halves which have different functions and have very different ways of processing information (see Figure 7.2). The two halves are linked by a complex network of nerve fibres called the *corpus collosum* which send messages from one side of the brain to the other. While the two halves do function together, research with patients in whom the link was severed revealed the two halves can function separately without communication with each other. When looking at the diagram (Figure 7.2), many people will recognize that they have a

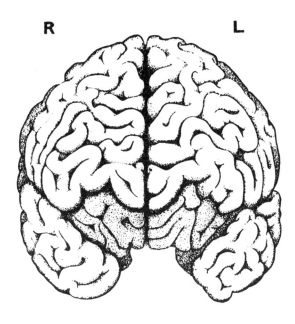

R   **L**

Figure 7.2 *Front view of the brain and its main functions*

stronger orientation to one side of the brain, in much the same way as they would recognize a preference for using their right or left hand. It is not yet certain how the two halves are coordinated. Neither half has a monopoly of a particular cognitive style, the functions being mainly one of emphasis.

The main implications for managers of this are:

- an awareness of one's own right or left brain orientation; and
- that it is possible to develop the weaker half. There are a number of techniques and exercises to develop both sides of the brain and interaction between them, which can constitute a self-development project. Most of us tend to have a stronger and more well-developed half and very few of us can claim the complete development and effective use and coordination of both halves. Einstein and Leonardo da Vinci are often quoted as good examples of well developed left and right brains.

Among managers in Western countries the left-hand side of the brain has become dominant. This is almost certainly due to a conditioning process. Western education and professional training and large organizations are all orientated to left-brain activities and indeed often reward them. At the extreme we tend to be dismissive and deride many of the specialisms of the right brain so that for many individuals it remains underdeveloped and underutilized. Step-by-step, logical, analytical thinkers are prized much more highly than holistic day-dreamers.

This state of affairs is beginning to change slowly for a number of reasons. First, there is the spread of self-improvement programmes which stress the importance of visualizing a positive self-image and striving to achieve it. The origins of these programmes lie in the science of 'psycho-cybernetics' first pioneered by Maxwell Maltz in the early 1960s. Cybernetics is the science of goal-achieving mechanisms and a cybernetic system operates by constantly receiving feedback on where it is so it can adjust accordingly in order to reach its target. A good example of such a system is a guided missile system. Psycho-cybernetics is therefore concerned with how the mind and body can combine toward the internal goal of an improved self-image; participants visualize an ultimate picture of themselves. Some of the techniques used utilize both the conscious and unconscious parts of the mind, and you start from knowing yourself before setting your goals.

Second, there is increasing recognition that in an unpredictable world of change, old solutions to new problems will not work. Creative thinking will be valued increasingly. According to Evans and Russell (1989), 'Organizations worldwide are beginning to realise that a key ingredient in responding to change is the development of people and their creativity'.

The need for creativity in managers has been recognized with the establishment of the Dupont Centre for Creativity in North Carolina, USA, where a number of key characteristics of creative thinkers have been identified:

- a discontent with the status quo
- offering alternative solutions to problems or opportunities
- continually alert to stimuli that might trigger ideas
- positive thinkers who work hard at thinking positively.

Third, there is increasing evidence that right-brain activity – intuition, insight, imagination, vision – are now contributing more and more to the decision-making processes of corporate leaders. Alder's study of CEOs in the UK revealed that they placed great emphasis on right-brain judgements and all possessed an ability to envision the future, a capability vital to corporate leadership. According to Alder (1994),

Manager 2000 would be able to see from other, new perspectives without losing the rational left-brain view. That is, he or she will have a balanced, multi-faceted or holistic view of what is going on – a way of thinking which harnesses the whole brain.

Right-brain thinking is not hereditary. It can be developed and its creative capacity harnessed. There are a number of techniques that can help us develop the brain, particularly the right-side; these include:

- *Mindmapping* – involves putting down on paper words, numbers, sequential items (left brain) and colours, images, symbols (right brain) in a random order around a certain theme or topic. Ideas are captured randomly and each one tends to lead to another. Ideas are usually recorded by lines and words so that the end product is like a tree with branches and twigs, each one containing a word. Random ideas are later grouped into a meaningful structure or framework. A speech, note-taking, an article, a book, often begin with a mindmap.

- *Brainstorming* – involves throwing ideas in a random way, usually in a group situation. At the creative stage, group members must not be judgemental or evaluative. Often the mildest idea can be the trigger for other ideas which will form the basis of future action.
- *Working in teams or action learning sets* – see Chapter 5.
- *Lateral thinking* – uses insights and creativity in a deliberate way to generate ideas that logical thinking cannot produce. It breaks out of old mind-sets and creates new thought patterns that give us more choices. Whereas logical or 'vertical' thinking is used to dig the same hole deeper, lateral thinking is used to dig a hole in another place. Whereas vertical thinking stops when it reaches a feasible solution, lateral thinking never stops searching for something better. And whereas vertical thinking has to proceed in logical steps, lateral thinking can produce the 'Eureka' effect – an insight unsupported by any logic. Some of the greatest scientific advances have resulted from lateral thinking.

Neuro-linguistic programming (NLP)

NLP is a set of techniques to help individuals change from mediocre to excellent performers. It helps people to think differently and positively so that it affects their behaviour and affects the behaviour of others. It teaches techniques for improved communication with ourselves and others and is part of an empowerment process for change and to enable us to take control of our lives.

This new development followed work in the USA in the 1970s by a linguistics specialist, Grinder, and mathematician, Bandler (1979). They made a comprehensive study of excellent practitioners in interpersonal communication, then identified the key factors contributing to this personal excellence and produced a model for one-to-one communication to assist others, combining skills of mathematical notation and linguistic analysis.

NLP is now being used widely in education, training and development and more recent work by Dilts and Grinder (1983) has extended the scope of NLP to leadership and the management of groups and organizations. The three words in the name give the key to defining it further:

neuro: refers to the neurological processes that we involve by using our five senses – seeing, hearing, feeling, smelling and tasting – which we use to experience our world. We use our brain as a filtering mechanism to arrive at our own subjective interpretation

linguistic: refers to how we organize our thoughts and express them through language. We express our thoughts both verbally and non-verbally

programming: refers to the way we programme our thoughts and behaviours to do things. From birth we learn to programme reactions and develop strategies which become internalized, lodged in our unconscious mind, and automatic.

By studying excellent performers, the researchers developed a framework to help individuals identify their own strategies and those of others. In short, it helps increase self-awareness and awareness of other strategies. From heightened self-awareness, individuals can choose whether to continue with their present automatic responses and behaviours, or begin a process of change.

NLP uses many different techniques some of which relate to self-management; an example is 'outcome thinking', which requires the subject to go through a number of stages.

- Thinking of a positive outcome associated with a certain situation and continually rehearsing it by imagining it through as many senses as possible.
- Identifying the personal resources such as confidence required to bring about a positive outcome, and to find those resources using stimulus/response techniques that require the individual to think of a time when he or she possessed that resource, to relive the emotions he or she experienced and to recall how he or she reached that state in order to help re-create it.
- Rehearsing the use of those resources in the new situation to try to ensure a positive outcome.

Such techniques have been used with sportsmen either to achieve success, or to avoid getting embroiled in future on-field troubles. For example, soccer players with a short temper who have been dismissed for retaliating to verbal and physical provocation are asked to visualize alternative responses in order to avoid future trouble.

Open learning

Sometimes called distance learning, this form of learning has enjoyed successful and spectacular growth since it was first pioneered in the UK by the Open University in the 1960s. There is no agreed definition of open learning, but it is based on the belief that it can open up new ways for adults to learn at a distance from the providing organization. Learning is usually a solitary activity, occasionally supplemented by group tutorials.

Open learning usually involves the use of specially prepared self-instructional materials or packages. These are often expensive to produce and buy. The packages are usually in modular form and can either 'stand alone' or be part of a complete course. Learners work through each module on a step-by-step basis and study or completion time can vary from a few hours for a single module to months or years for a complete course.

Open learning is *one* self-development method and its main advantages are:

- it is very flexible as to how and when it can be used
- it requires little time off work – individuals usually work on packages in their own time
- its modular structure enables individuals to progress on a 'step-by-step' basis with opportunities for reinforcement and clarification
- it is less threatening because there is little or no group exposure. This can be very appealing to those with a low self-concept, perhaps caused by limited formal educational qualifications.

There have been many impressive achievements through open learning by those with little formal education, often of mature years, which have resulted in improved self-confidence, job competence and career progression. Also, the relatively low cost of tutorial support can make it a much cheaper alternative to other training and development opportunities.

There are, of course, some disadvantages:

- some of the packages, especially in the field of computer-based training and interactive video, are extremely expensive
- good personal discipline and study habits are required, which some people may not possess
- learner isolation can have adverse motivational effects, so that some programmes are characterized by a high drop-out rate
- there is little opportunity for peer support or peer learning.

An open learning package can be a useful self-development tool that offers flexibility and at times cost-effectiveness. It will rarely offer many of the wider benefits of group learning, but nevertheless, many individuals can show impressive results from its use.

Career development

A 'career' is defined by the *Oxford English Dictionary* as 'a person's progress through life, a profession offering opportunities for advancement'. There will probably be little argument with the first part, but there may have to be some reappraisal about advancement. Flatter structures and reduced hierarchies in the wake of widespread down-sizing operations have ensured that steady hierarchical progression is no longer guaranteed. Managers may therefore have to settle for a career where they broaden their skills and knowledge and where they assume different responsibilities, but not in the traditional hierarchical sense.

For reasons of both career advancement and job satisfaction, it is important not to stay too long in one job. A balance between change for change's sake and sinking into a deep rut needs to be struck. Change therefore needs to be planned and progressive so that each new situation brings an element of novelty and challenge that can be coped with. As a rule of thumb, you should look for a job change every three to four years, especially in the early years of a career. It is especially important that those wanting to make the transition from technical expert to manager do not leave the change too late and that once the change is made, a variety and depth of experience is sought. The learning from each move needs to be processed to improve your own development.

In terms of seeking new opportunities it is important in the present age that individuals take the initiative to seek fresh opportunities. The days of working in a paternalistic organization and waiting for the call to better things have gone. New opportunities need to be discovered and the individual must make things happen rather than just let them happen. A range of fresh opportunities can be provided in the following ways.

Exchanges

This is where one person exchanges jobs with another for a period of time ranging from three to 12 months. They are widely used in the education sector, often on an international basis. If properly managed they are an invaluable way of gaining experience, to which the author can testify. There needs to be proper induction and appropriate guidance and support, particularly during the early stages when the participant is struggling to come to terms with the new environment.

Just as individuals should be encouraged to process the experience and learn accordingly, so organizations should attempt the same and bring participants together on a regular basis so they can learn from one another. In many cases such experience is wasted and valuable lessons that could be implemented are lost.

Secondments

This involves an individual being seconded to another area or field for a period of time for anything up to a year. Again, they are prevalent in the education sector and also in organizations which have a high emphasis on project management, such as construction. Sometimes secondment can be to an overseas location.

Like exchanges, secondments offer excellent learning and development opportunities, but they should also carry a strong health warning. Re-entry, especially if it involves repatriation, can be a very painful process, and participants should recognize that both they and the organization have 'moved on' – and not necessarily in tandem. Re-entry is a time for reappraisal and therefore the individual must either renegotiate his or her position within the organization or consider moving elsewhere.

Job rotation

This involves either a requested move within an organization or an organizationally imposed one at prescribed intervals in order to gain experience. The latter is very common in the armed services. All changes bring some disruption to family life, so any move needs to be carefully timed.

Representing the organization

Requests are made regularly to organizations to make presentations about their work. These can take various forms such as talking to schools and community groups, presenting at conferences, or appearing on local radio and TV. Such requests can be viewed as a development opportunity and the organization has a vested interest in its representative making a successful appearance. Such appearances can do immense good (or harm!) to the organization's image as well as the confidence levels of the representative(s). Such appearances should be carefully managed to maximize the chances of positive outcomes.

Contributing to community groups

Community service can offer a valuable self-development tool. Experience can be gained that may not be available within the confines of the workplace, and the opportunity for cross-fertilization between different sectors is always valuable. Examples of this kind of experience could be managers from the industrial sector serving on the board of governors of schools and colleges, or taking a committee position with a local sports club.

Summary

Some of the main points in this chapter.

- Self-development involves personal change – new knowledge, new abilities, new skills, new feelings and different outlooks – and responsibility for this rests with the individual.
- Individuals need to obtain objective feedback from several external sources to help assess their own development needs, after which they need to contract with themselves a number of realistic goals.
- Self-development embraces developing competences as a manager or supervisor, developing personal skills which may or may not be required in the present job, and seeking opportunities outside the scope of the present job to help meet career aspirations.
- There is a large range of self-development opportunities. These exist in both the workplace and in our leisure time. It is important that the lessons of experience are properly processed in order to maximize learning.

References and further reading

Alder, H (1993) *The Right Brain Manager*, London: Piatkus.

Alder, H (1994) *NLP: The new art and science of getting what you want*, London: Piatkus.

Bandler, R and Grinder, J (1979) *Frogs Into Princes*, London: Real People Press.

Buzan, T (1982) *Use Your Head*, London: BBC Publications.

Buzan, T (1988) *Make the Most of Your Mind*, London: Cold Books.

De Bono, E (1977) *Lateral Thinking*, Harmondsworth: Penguin.

Dilts, R (1983) *Applications of Neuro-Linguistic Programming*, Cupertino, California: Meta Publications.

Evans, R and Russell, P (1989) *The Creative Manager*, London: Unwin.

Francis, D and Woodcock, M (1982) *The Unblocked Manager. A practical guide to self-development*, Aldershot: Gower.

Francis, D and Woodcock, M (1982) *50 Activities for Self-Development*, Aldershot: Gower.

Honey, P (1990) 'Confessions of a learner who is inclined to lapse', *Training & Development Journal*, June.

Maltz, M (1960) *Psycho Cybernetics*, New York: Simon & Schuster.

Maslow, A H (1968) *Towards a Psychology of Being*, New York: Van Nostrand.

Megginson, D and Pedler, M (1991) *Developing the Developers*, London: AMED.

Megginson, D and Pedler, M (1992) *Self-development. A facilitator's guide*, Maidenhead: McGraw-Hill.

Mumford A (1986) 'Learning to learn for managers', *Journal of Management Development*, 10, 2.

O'Connor, J and Seymour, J (1990) *Introducing Neurolinguistic Programming*, London: Harper Collins.

Ornstein, R (1978) *The Split and Whole Brain*, Human Nature 1, pp. 76–83.

Pedler, M, Burgoyne, J and Boydell, T (1986) *A Manager's Guide to Self-Development*, (2nd edn), Maidenhead: McGraw-Hill.

Pedler, M, Burgoyne, J and Boydell, T (1988) *Applying Self-development in Organisations*, Hemel Hempstead: Prentice Hall.

Robbins, A (1986) *Unlimited Power*, London: Simon & Schuster.

Robbins, A (1992) *Awaken the Giant Within*, London: Simon & Schuster.

Shane, R (1984) *Creative Visualisation*, Wellingborough: Thorsons.

Smith, R M (1983) *Learning How to Learn: Applied theory to adults*, Milton Keynes: Open University Press.

Sperry, R W (1966) 'Brain Bisection and Consciousness', in *Brain and Conscious Experience*, J Eccles (ed), New York: Springer-Verlag.

Sperry, R W (1974) 'Lateral Specialisation in the Surgically Separated Hemispheres', in *The Neurosciences Third Study Program*, FO Schmitt & FC Worden (eds), Cambridge, MA: MIT Press.

Storne, R (1984) *Creative Visualisation. How to use imagery and imagination for self improvement*, Wellingborough: Thorsons.

Chapter 8

Counselling and Coaching

The degree to which I can create relationships which facilitate the growth of others as separate persons is a measure of the growth I have achieved myself. In some respects this is a disturbing thought, but it is also a promising or challenging one. It would indicate that if I am interested in creating helping relationships I have a fascinating lifetime job ahead of me, stretching and developing my potentialities in the direction of growth. (Rogers, 1961)

Definition of counselling

The ability to counsel and to establish a counselling relationship is now an important prerequisite and additional skill to becoming an effective manager in the modern age. Years ago when disciples of scientific management, Taylorism and Theory X (people naturally hate work and responsibility; they need to be coerced and directed from above) were widely in evidence in management positions, attributes of empathy, understanding, etc were not held to be of great importance. As humanistic psychology comes of age with an increasing realization of the contribution it can make to more effective management, then the counselling skill and its benefits are becoming more appreciated.

The above quote from Rogers emphasizes that the helping relationship is beneficial and developmental for both parties. While the person being counselled will (hopefully) benefit as a result of achieving some acceptable solution to a problem, the counsellor will benefit also from developing a wide range of interpersonal skills plus confidence in handling a person in a helping, and often difficult, situation. When a student takes pride and satisfaction in examination success and achievement, their teacher shares similar feelings and achievement; this parallels the counselling relationship.

There is no one, universally accepted definition of counselling, but the following should give a firm indication of its scope:

> the task of counselling is to give the client an opportunity to explore, discover and clarify ways of living more resourcefully and towards greater well-being. (British Association of Counselling, 1988)

> a set of techniques, skills and attitudes to help people manage their own problems using their own resources. (Reddy, 1987)

> the skilled and principal use of relationship to facilitate self-knowledge, emotional acceptance and growth, and the optimal development of personal resources. (British Association of Counselling, 1992)

While for most of the time most people can deal with their own problems, everyone at some stage of their life is in need of help. No man is an island and no one is in the situation where they will never need the help of others. The range of problems is very wide and a leading counselling agency gave the following categories (not in order of frequency):

- employment, eg, redundancy, dismissal, relocation, long-term sick leave, relationships with colleagues, especially the boss
- physical, eg, AIDS/HIV, disability, terminal illness
- emotional, eg, depression, anxiety, threatened/attempted suicide, trauma
- family, eg, aged parents, child abuse, violence in the home
- marital, eg, divorce, separation
- relationships, eg, partners, neighbours, racial/sexual harassment
- property loss, eg, burglary, flood, fire
- substance misuse, eg, alcohol, drugs
- finance, eg, debt, bankruptcy
- bereavement/loss
- housing, eg, repossession, homelessness
- crime, eg, arrest, prosecution, victim of crime.

In addition, counselling or aspects of the counselling skill may be required with performance issues at work and with the appraisal process. More and more organizations are developing and implementing appraisal schemes and a key factor in determining their success relates to the ability of the manager to conduct an appraisal interview.

It must be stressed in the strongest possible terms that I am not advocating that all managers become expert counsellors, but I am advocating that managers:

- develop an awareness and use of basic counselling skills which will probably be used in appraisal interviewing and may be used to address minor problems relating to other employees
- become aware of the power of counselling and its benefits
- become aware of their own limitations and know when to request external help. The well intentioned Samaritan who gets out of his or her depth will do more harm than good.

Benefits of counselling

In a more enlightened era, many organizations are waking up to the positive benefits of counselling and realizing that it can impact on personal effectiveness and the bottom line. Also, management attitudes have changed and the old-school autocratic style of management has largely petered out. Attitudes revealed in such clichés as the following have largely been consigned to history:

If they don't perform, sack 'em.

Pull yourself together, man.

We don't tolerate softies around here.

Asking for help is a sign of weakness.

I tell 'em straight – they know where they stand with me.

Benefits can be seen for both the individual and the organization.

The individual

Counselling can help people with their personal problems which may range from severe to minor. In fact, with some of the latter, there may not be a problem as such; they may merely need the opportunity to talk to someone and put the issue in perspective. For example, a psychiatrist's analysis of worries about which he had been consulted revealed:

40 per cent: things that never happen
30 per cent: things that have happened and cannot be changed
12 per cent: illnesses and other things that never materialized
10 per cent: children and friends who were able to help themselves
8 per cent: real problems.

We all need to unload on someone else at some time and merely finding a sympathetic ear can be positively therapeutic. At the other end of the spectrum, real problems do exist and the owner may need careful and sensitive handling. Personal problems require greater empathy than technical problems, which can often be solved by telling or advising. Helping an individual to solve a personal problem reduces individual unhappiness or discontent and increases personal efficiency. It is also a satisfying time for the helper and will usually improve the relationship beyond recognition. In the case of the manager-subordinate relationship the benefits are multiplied and may show themselves in increased motivation, reduced tension and conflict and improved team-working.

A client-centred counselling process usually results in decisions that are owned and often implemented. The counsellor has not told the client the solution but has merely helped them to decide the option to follow. Such an approach takes more time than telling, but once a decision has been reached, ownership usually guarantees commitment.

A positive outcome to a positive process often results in human growth for both parties. The client realizes that they can see things differently and they are capable of thinking for themselves. Problems may even be positively perceived as opportunities and the techniques and mental skills applied during the process may be transferable elsewhere. Change for the better can result. As Egan (1962) states:

Since interpersonal helping is such a common human experience, one wonders whether some kind of training in helping shouldn't be as common as training in reading, writing and math. ... training in helping skills could benefit all interpersonal helpers: parents, in managing marital problems and in helping their children grow and develop; friends in helping loved ones in times of trouble; and individuals in helping themselves to cope more creatively with the problems of life.

The client-centred approach is very much in tune with the spirit of the 1990s in which increasing emphasis is on self-development and empowering people to take more and more responsibility for themselves and their future. Most of us need help and support at varying stages on this journey and often this can come from a manager. Facilitating the growth and development of subordinates and empowering them to both cope with and implement change is an increasingly important managerial function.

The organization

Every organization is a complex web of intricate social systems containing numerous formal choices of authority. Everybody in the organization has a reporting relationship, in all cases formal, and in some cases an additional informal reporting relationship. Organizations operate on a manager-subordinate relationship, and the healthier this relationship is, the healthier the organization and the more effective the employees. Conversely, the poorer the relationship, the more ineffective and unproductive will employees be.

Relationship difficulties or personality clashes are, as stated earlier, one of the main problems requiring interventions. The vast majority occur because of a breakdown in communication which may manifest itself in a variety of ways, such as avoiding, manipulating and dominating behaviours. A counselling type relationship will go a long way towards improving a problem relationship and, if it is beyond repair, it can help in the search for more productive alternatives. Too often individuals are unable to confront the situation, operating instead behind each other's back rather than in the open, and usually making an already difficult situation even worse. Confronting a difficult situation requires courage on both sides, but usually the longer the situation is ignored or avoided, the worse the problem becomes.

Thus, if we can move to a situation where the culture or climate of an organization encourages openness in interpersonal communication, then over a period of time there will inevitably be a reduction in the number of relationship difficulties, creating a healthier organizational climate. In short, counselling can unblock a lot of blocked organizational communication channels.

The encouragement of 'helping relationships' among individuals must be viewed long-term rather than short-term. For many this will involve a change in attitudes, behaviours, traditions and values, which is difficult and for some, impossible. Such a long-term view of improving interpersonal relationships can be seen as a valuable 'organizational development' (OD) method. OD is a very inexact science which came to the fore in the late 1960s and 1970s and while there is no universally accepted definition, it has been closely related to change and how organizations can implement change and adapt to it. Counselling, therefore, can be an extremely effective way of coming to terms with change and implementing it.

Organizations are made up of people who have aspirations and ambitions, and many who seek to achieve their full potential. Many employees are frustrated in their efforts and feel that organizations constrain potential rather than encourage it. Counselling may help individuals achieve their potential. It may take place in a formal situation such as the appraisal interview, but it may also take place on numerous informal occasions. Whatever the occasion, successful outcomes depend on how the process is handled. Usually the less the manager has to use the authority of role and the more informal the process, the better will be the outcome.

Organizations should be providing the means to help people develop and these means often extend well beyond the provision of a course. There are an increasing number of opportunities available for workplace learning and often the real learning and development accrues from the processing of the experience. Counselling will often help individuals to gain insight into their own experiences and learnings. This is because the counsellor can reflect back information in an objective way, so helping the client to understand and move forward.

Every day in the workplace there are individuals who are not performing to their capabilities because they are being adversely affected by a personal problem. A list of the major categories was given earlier in the chapter; many of these can be resolved quite quickly by counselling. Richard Chiumento of Chiumento Counselling Group believes that only 20 per cent of problems require more than two or three counselling sessions. For very little cost, a problem can be quickly resolved with the result that an employee returns to a more productive and effective level of output. Extra individual productivity should quickly recoup the counselling cost for the organization.

It is for this reason that numerous organizations in the USA and UK have implemented an Employee Assistance Programme (EAP), using external counselling services. Many such programmes have claimed impressive results. It is beyond the scope of this chapter to discuss EAPs but they are an indication of managers and organizations waking up to the benefit of counselling and the contribution it can make to individual effectiveness and personal and organization development.

The counselling relationship

All three definitions of counselling given earlier have a couple of common themes:

- that responsibility for the problem and solution(s) rests with the client
- that the counsellor forms a relationship with the client to help them become more resourceful in addressing their difficulties.

An elaboration of Figure 8.1 will reveal more clearly how this works. The diagram follows the three-stage model of exploration – understanding – action developed by Carkhuff (1983).

People with a problem usually have difficulty in resolving it on their own. Their experience in fields relating to the problem may be limited, they may be too close to the problem to be objective and they may be so emotionally involved that they lose all sense of perspective. Clarity of thought can be impeded by anxiety, fear, etc., and there appears no way forward.

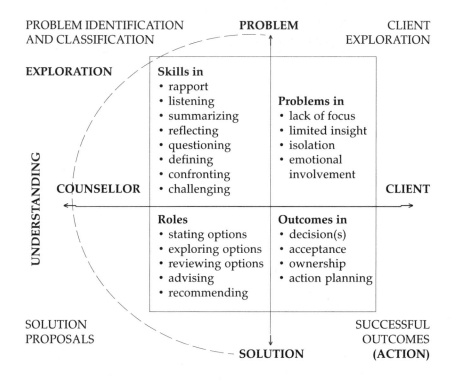

PROBLEM IDENTIFICATION
AND CLASSIFICATION

EXPLORATION

PROBLEM

CLIENT
EXPLORATION

Figure 8.1 *The dimensions of the counselling relationship*

Asking for help is not a weakness but a sign of strength in that we are being open about our limitations and the need for greater resources, but once the step of asking for help has been taken we need to respect the counsellor both as a person and for their contribution.

From the counsellor's point of view, such respect will be built up over a period of time and gradually the client will confide more and more in them. Egan (1962) states that skilful counsellors build respect by following these principles:

- they exhibit genuine concern for the person and the problem. They do not use the situation for manipulation, personal gain or as an arena to impose their own agenda;
- they are clear communicators and the messages sent are clearly understood;
- they are in tune with people's feelings and can judge their state of mind;
- they are prepared for uncovering uncomfortable facts or

143

feelings without losing their respect for the client or impairing their judgement; and

- they are open-minded and non-judgemental.

Some of the skills required of a skilful counsellor are as follows:

- the ability to establish support with the client. Any first meeting will usually involve some feelings of anxiety, vulnerability, etc, which need to be diffused early in the relationship. A continual process of self-disclosure begins on both sides, especially for the client, which will continue during the relationship. Early on a process of contracting will begin which will involve clarifying expectations and outcomes wanted from the session;
- the ability to listen and empathize;
- the ability to both summarize and reflect, ie, check understanding of facts and feelings and clarify exactly what they are;
- the ability to use appropriate questioning technique, especially open and probing questions;
- confronting the real issues and challenging the client on those issues;
- the ability to facilitate the listing and evaluation of options;
- giving advice and recommending where appropriate but leaving the final decision to the client; telling, is also usually avoided.

The counselling relationship should hopefully result in positive outcomes in which the client accepts, owns and is committed to the decisions made and will be able to implement the decisions within an acceptable and agreed time-frame. While a client-centred approach is much more time-consuming, this commitment allied to little loss of personal worth and self-esteem on the part of the client, ensures a better and more permanent outcome.

Implementing counselling skills in an organization

Organizations that decide to improve the level of counselling skills among some of its managers will need to start with a training programme in basic counselling skills. This should aim to give managers both the skills and confidence to assist people to clarify and define for themselves ways of coping more effectively in a number of situations. It will not equip managers to deal with advanced cases requiring specialist training, although for the few, it may provide the platform to progress to more in-depth training.

A basic three-day programme such as the one outlined below, should give managers:

- an understanding of the different ways of helping others;
- a greater self-awareness and understanding of how to develop self-awareness;
- awareness of individual limitations and the opportunity to identify when to refer on to others;
- an opportunity to identify and practise the basic skills of counselling; and
- a working knowledge of where the ethical boundaries lie.

In outline form the course would appear similar to the following.

Day 1

Introductions. Needs. Expectations
What is counselling? The three-stage model (see Figure 8.1)
The skills of exploration – explanation and practice
Framework for the first interview
Awareness exercises
Learning review

Day 2

Review of day 1
The skills of understanding and proposing – explanation and practice
Attachment, loss and endings
Awareness exercises
Learning review

Day 3

Review of day 2
The skills of stage 3 – explanation and practice
Ethics, boundaries and good practice
Recognizing and dealing with stressful situations
Endings and application
Learning review and action planning
Closing plenary.

A follow-up day, three to six months after the course, is recommended. This would give participants the opportunity to meet in order to share, compare and advise each other on their experiences to date.

Giving feedback

Earlier in the chapter a comprehensive list of situations in which individuals may request or require help was given, some of which will require skills beyond those of the line manager. While this chapter has agreed for a client-centred approach to the counselling situation, there are a number of additional occasions when a manager will have to give feedback; such occasions could include:

- during an appraisal interview when a subordinate's performance is being reviewed;
- when there are performance problems;
- during a development centre, an event at which line managers take on the role of coach/counsellor;
- giving feedback from psychometric instruments;
- during career discussions and planning; and
- giving feedback at team or group meetings either in the work situation or on a course.

The end goals of feedback should be:

- acceptance and ownership of the feedback by the recipient;
- a commitment to change, where appropriate; and
- some discussion, however preliminary, of follow-up action.

There are a number of guidelines to help in giving feedback; these include:

- ensure that there is privacy and no distractions so that you can devote yourself entirely to giving feedback;
- take time to establish rapport and try to empathize with the other person;
- try to be open and honest with your feedback and closely observe the impact it is having on the recipient;
- use clear, concise language;
- avoid being judgemental. Focus on fact, not opinion, by giving specific behavioural feedback. Let the final evaluation come from the recipient;
- offer yourself or others as a resource to help the recipient change, when appropriate. Giving feedback that requires change which is beyond the resources of the recipient without any offer of support is of limited value;
- check for understanding at regular intervals, particularly at the end; and
- try and finish on a positive note, looking forward rather than backwards. Some managers find it very difficult to make positive comments. It is just as important to focus on the positive as on the negative or developmental.

Learning the skills of giving feedback greatly increases an individual's value as a person and as a manager and to the organization. As line managers have an increasing role to play in developing others, the acquisition of feedback skills will be an important prerequisite to this role.

Informal networks

People in organizations usually develop informal networks that co-exist alongside the formal lines of authority. They usually consist of people from different functions and have no formal lines of authority. They can, at times, offer a very useful form of support to a person in need. Managers who have developed some counselling skills will be in a position to deal more effectively with these requests or situations when they occur.

Definition of coaching

The best place to start a section on coaching is with a couple of definitions of the term which can then be used to develop some of the key characteristics of this approach:

> Systematically increasing the ability and the experience of the trainee by giving him or her planned tasks coupled with continuous appraisal advice and counselling by the trainee's supervisor. (Manpower Services Commission, 1981)

> The release of latent talent and skills, previously untapped by training, through a process of self-awareness initiated by the coach. (Salisbury, 1994)

There are a number of distinctive characteristics of coaching that separate it from both training and counselling; these are discussed below.

As a general rule, trainers have to be competent in the area in which they are training. Usually the level of skill possessed by the trainer exceeds the level of skill possessed by the trainees. With coaching this may *not* be the case. While some knowledge of the job or subject is important, a coach does not have to be proficient, or expert, in what is being coached and certainly may not be more skilful than the person receiving coaching. The world of top-class sport demonstrates this point admirably. Many young tennis players and golfers are coached by people whose skill level is much lower. In fact, outstanding exponents of a skill rarely make good coaches, not least because they lack the patience and perseverance to devote the required amount of time with lesser mortals. The skills and attributes of a good coach are very different from those of a good trainer.

The primary goal of coaching is the achievement of individual potential. This contrasts with the primary goal of training which is to give a person the basic skills in order to meet the required standard or to do the job satisfactorily.

Thus training comes before coaching and is the starting point to equip people with the skills to cope. Coaching helps people go beyond the basic requirements to release skills that have not yet been released. In other words, it enables individuals to develop their potential and often to the full.

Coaching may therefore not be concerned with excellence:

the person being coached may not be excellent or the very best. But coaching is concerned with helping an individual achieve the best they are capable of. Many school children today receive private coaching in order to reach the required standard for exams, their parents recognizing that additional help is needed.

At the other end of the spectrum, coaching can enable the excellent performer to get even better and for the highest achievers, new and better levels of performance are a constant goal. Olympic athletes continually strive to be not only the best, but to be the best ever, and in their quest rely heavily on their personal coach.

Coaching must be viewed as a long-term event for both the individual and for organizations who adopt it as a training and development method. Coaching aims for continuous improvement by setting a series of goals. Each successive goal should be challenging but attainable. Success in achieving a goal provides the motivation to aim for achieving the next.

As with counselling, coaching places the responsibility for performance improvement with the individual, ie, the person being coached. The main responsibility of the coach is the provision of support in the appropriate form. Skills of facilitating, enabling and giving feedback are very much to the fore. Feedback skills are especially important as self-awareness is a vital requisite for success, and the coach is the main source of feedback. It is for this reason that closed circuit television is used in sports coaching and team development workshops, so that the coach's feedback can be reinforced by evidence of what actually happened.

Coaching is usually done with small numbers and is often very individualized. A one-to-one relationship is very common. This enables the coach and pupil the opportunity to build up a long-term relationship, while at the same time giving the coach a unique insight and understanding of what motivates an individual and the type of approach to adopt in order to achieve success.

Benefits of coaching

In an organizational setting, the applications and benefits of coaching are wide and varied. It is just as beneficial for people who are new to a job as it can be for employees with a long service record. People in a job go through a number of distinct stages as they ascend the learning curve; these are shown below in Figure 8.2.

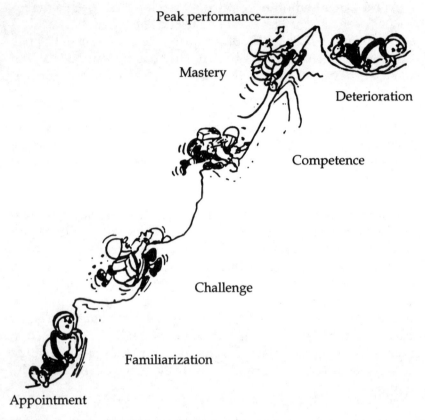

Figure 8.2 *The learning curve in a job*

Stage 1: Familiarization

The post-holder goes through a relatively short period of familiarizing him or her self with the new situation. This period is probably longer with an appointment to a new organization, where time is required to tune-in to the new ways of doing things, a new culture, new systems and procedures. It is a period in which individual productivity is low, and it tends to be longer in large organizations, where the costs of a period of low productivity can be more easily absorbed.

Stage 2: Challenge

This is a demanding stage that stretches the individual, often to full capacity. Credibility has to be established and relationships forged and this takes time. Tasks take longer to accomplish as the best way of working needs to be learned.

Stage 3: Competence

By trial and error learning the individual develops in the job. Both mistakes and successes are used as learning opportunities, and the time taken to complete a task is reduced. Relationships continue to be built, the circle of contacts is widened and credibility rises.

Stage 4: Mastery

This stage is characterized by acceptance and credibility in the organization. The formal and informal systems and procedures are well known so the minimum time is expended on routine matters. Key tasks can often be completed more quickly and to a high standard as a result of accumulated experience. As a rule of thumb, it will probably take an individual in a managerial position between three and five years to reach this stage, at which point the post-holder will begin to think about the next job and will look for wider possibilities and opportunities.

Stage 5: Determination

This begins to occur when an individual has been in the job too long. The job ceases to offer the challenge, stimulation and satisfaction it once did and the incumbent is unable or unwilling to find fresh challenges. Dissatisfaction and boredom can manifest itself in numerous behaviours such as lack of cooperation, obstructiveness and refusal or inability to adopt to change. Some find other outlets and challenge energies and creativity into activities outside of work. Responsibility for allowing an individual to reach and atrophy at this stage rests with the individual and the organization.

Coaching can be used with individuals at all stages of the learning curve and can offer several benefits to the organization:

- it can allow individuals to improve their performance on the job. In the case of employees at the foot of the learning curve, coaching can shorten the length of Stage 2 so that the organization gets a quicker return on the cost of employing a relatively new recruit. At the top end of the curve, developing employees with a longer service record as coaches may offer the challenge and stimulation they are seeking, plus it ensures that years of accumulated experience are passed on to others
- it can enable individuals who possess the potential to deliver an excellent performance. People usually have greater aspirations than a manager realizes and most want to be excellent performers. The difference between those who perform to a high standard and those that do not is usually the manager. Managers who operate as coaches can help people become excellent performers
- it opens up the communication channels between manager and subordinate, usually making for improved relationships. Good relationships make for a better and more productive working environment
- the costs are low, so that a return on investment should soon be evident.

Problems in developing coaches

The effectiveness of a coaching approach can be reduced by a number of factors. Thorough planning, commitment and training can reduce or eliminate the impact of these factors, which include:

- lack of senior management support, without which progress will be limited. Senior management need to be sold the benefits in order to get commitment

- managers finding it difficult to let go of the reins of management. Losing control can be uncomfortable and threatening for many managers. Many of the principles of good delegation need to be adopted, such as getting the right match of assignment and individual, supporting the subordinate and monitoring progress. Line managers who act as coaches are ultimately accountable for the performance of individuals and teams within their work area. Good coaching should ensure high performance from both
- the wrong choice of managers as coaches. Just because people are managers, it does not mean they have the capabilities or potential to be coaches. Organizations are rife with managers who have good administrative skills but poorly developed people skills. It is wrongly assumed that such managers will make good coaches
- managers adopting an inappropriate style. Much of coaching involves 'letting go': supporting and helping the subordinate develop through a gradual process of self-awareness. Many managers find this difficult, adopting a firm and directive 'telling' style which, while on occasions is appropriate, can cause problems. As with counselling, some basic training and regular follow-up meetings are recommended
- managers new to coaching making the mistake of trying to do too much all at once and expecting too much too quickly. In coaching you have to be prepared for setbacks and lack of progress from time to time. More support and encouragement is required from the coach during these difficult periods. It is worth remembering that over a period of time, while the level of skill acquisition and performance will increase, the curve is not a smooth one of constant improvement. The curve is one of improvement, plateau-ing and occasional regressions and it is during the latter stages when the support of the coach is particularly important.

The requirements of a good coach

Some of the requirements of a good coach incorporate those of a good trainer and counsellor, with one or two extras. The requirements include:

- the ability to listen, observe and diagnose, and knowing when to interrupt;
- an understanding of human nature and psychology. This is important in such areas as motivation, skill acquisition and goal setting;
- recognizing the importance of individual feelings and knowing when to spend time dealing with these rather than directing efforts towards improved performance;
- having awareness of one's own strengths and weaknesses. Self-awareness training, as in counselling, is recommended;
- a caring, supportive and patient nature. Often progress may not be as quick as both sides would want; and
- good verbal skills, especially in the area of feedback.

Lessons from the world of sport

In the field of coaching there is much to be learnt from sport. The principles, techniques and methods can often be applied to coaching in the workplace. The following transcript is a record of an interview I conducted with John Malfait. John was instrumental in founding and developing the Northamptonshire Cricket Association coaching scheme for young players in the 1980s. He is a National Cricket Association staff coach employed by MCC as assistant to the head coach at the MCC Indoor Cricket School at Lord's Cricket Ground, London.

The school offers coaching for young cricketers from the age of 8, through to many of the world's top test match cricketers. The range of abilities and needs is therefore vast.

TP: Thank you for agreeing to be interviewed. What I want to talk about is coaching and really the *principles* of coaching, because it seems to me that, having been a coach in cricket, there are many principles that can be applied from cricket to the world of business and management. Before moving on to these principles, can you briefly describe to me the job you do at Lord's?

JM: I am the Assistant to the MCC Head Coach, Clive Radley, the former England and Middlesex batsman. My responsibilities relate to the Indoor School. I produce the syllabus and programme for all the coaching courses that take place at the Indoor School and this includes the content of each course and the organization of the coaches, many of whom have first class playing experience.

TP: What levels of ability do you coach?

JM: My job is extremely varied. It is not unusual to be coaching an eight-year old, an adult player of limited ability, and a top professional on the same day – each of whom demands a very different approach.

TP: In other words, a very wide range of ability.

JM: Yes – very wide.

TP: How would you define coaching?

JM: Coaching takes place in all avenues of life – in business, in music, in the arts, and of course, in sport. It occurs whenever someone is willing to share their experience, their knowledge and their expertise with other people. Coaching involves verbal instruction, visual demonstrations, guidance and a sound understanding of human nature.

TP: What would you say are the main benefits of coaching?

JM: To be effective coaching sessions must be well planned and structured to meet the needs of the participants. Coaching is not just about producing top performers – it should also encourage people of all abilities to enjoy their sport and help them achieve their potential. Good coaching will teach technique, develop skills, instil confidence and improve awareness of the sport. Coaches should be prepared to invest time and effort seeking ways to extend their knowledge, skills and expertise to ensure maximum benefit for all.

TP: So there is very much a developmental aspect in coaching for the coaches themselves? Both coach and pupil have a learning curve to ascend?

JM: That's right. I rarely run a course where I don't learn something, either from other coaches or from course members. It might easily come from working with little eight-year-olds – something might happen and I think, 'My goodness, I can use that' or, 'That's an interesting development' or, 'I can build that into my repertoire as a coach'.

TP: What are the basic skills required for coaching?

JM: The coach requires the ability to plan, organize and

manage efficiently and these are just three of the many skills a good coach is expected to possess. Coaches must be able to communicate effectively and it is prudent to recognize that good listening is a key factor in effective communication, and its importance is often overlooked.

Information and instructions to participants, parents and others needs to be delivered in a clear and concise manner. All coaches should have a comprehensive knowledge of the techniques, skills, tactics, laws and rules of their sport.

A good coach is capable of presenting accurate visual skill demonstrations and is able to identify the relevant strengths and weaknesses of individual performers. Leadership and man management skills, together with an ability to motivate and encourage, are also valuable attributes that good coaches possess.

TT: Another very important aspect of coaching is goal setting. Is there anything you would like to say about that?

JM: Goal setting is very important. Skilful goal setting can motivate and instil confidence in individuals, teams or even squads. Effective goal setting needs to be well planned with clearly defined areas – immediate, short term, long term.

Perhaps the most fundamental skill in goal setting is the ability to focus the attention of participants towards an appropriate goal, and sometimes it is useful to encourage the setting of self targets, such as so many runs or wickets in a season. Achieving these landmarks builds confidence.

Other goals can be set. For example, batsmen who lack concentration can set a goal of batting until 11.20am and then until 11.40am and so on. In other words, goals related to time. In the longer term targets can be set, such as so many runs or wickets per season. All these are things a coach can help a player with, because it is often the mental side of the game rather than physical side that creates problems.

Goals either physical or mental should be designed to create a realistic challenge – they need to be meaningful and difficult enough to extend, but easy enough to attain.

Skilful, realistic goal setting will motivate and instil

confidence. Unrealistic, unattainable goals will demotivate and may well cause a decline in confidence and performance.

TP: I should think in your job you have experienced the 'highs' and the 'lows'. Can you give me an example of a satisfying success?

JM: Yes. Over the last few years it has been immensely satisfying to watch the spectacular progress of youngsters associated with the Northamptonshire Cricket Association (NCA), many of whom are now on the playing staff of the Northamptonshire County Cricket Club.

A memory I shall always treasure is the moment at Lord's Cricket ground in August 1991 when two young men from Northamptonshire, Mal Loye and Russell Warren, walked down the famous pavilion steps at Lord's to open the England Under 19 innings against Australia – having assisted, together with other local NCA volunteer coaches, in their development – that moment at Lord's was indeed very satisfying, very emotional and made me feel very proud.

Coaching provides many magical moments and it is always a great thrill to see the delight on the face of a young boy who has suddenly mastered a specific skill. He may never become a professional cricketer, but achievement at any level is satisfying and dreams do sometimes come true.

TP: So what you are saying is that coaching can bring a great deal of inner satisfaction from helping people develop and achieve a milestone?

JM: Absolutely.

TP: That's the success side of it, John. What about a failure?

JM: Disappointments – there are a few – such as individuals who, through lack of self discipline and outside distractions, have failed to reach their true potential. It is also disappointing when young performers fall by the wayside through lack of guidance and opportunity.

TP: So you have to be prepared for your failures or disappointments, even though you may be working with good material?

JM: Yes.

TP: For those aspiring to become a coach, is there any advice you would give them?

JM: Enthusiasm and a good knowledge of their sport and its techniques, together with a genuine desire to help participants enjoy their sport and improve performance are sound principles for all coaches to follow.

It is wise to recognize that most people respond favourably to praise and encouragement – few are encouraged by negative criticism.

Coaches should have the ability to assess, identify and understand the needs of participants and coach accordingly. It is no good coaching a 13-year-old as if he is a test match player, and vice versa.

You therefore need to assess the situation and coach in an appropriate way. I think man management is important and to get the confidence of the person you are coaching. He needs to believe in you and you have to put it over to him that you believe in him as well and instil confidence and make people believe they can do it and not look on the failures. The latter is an important part of coaching and coaches do sometimes look on the failures when people don't do well. It is much better to get a good balance and encourage.

Another point is that a coach must recognize, and get a player to recognize, his limitations and try to play within those limitations. In other words, play to his strengths and there are many players who have done just that and been very successful.

Finally, it must be remembered that all coaching sessions should be safe, enjoyable and instructive.

TP: You mentioned there the importance of a knowledge of the game and a knowledge of good technique. But it also seems to me there are other dimensions to coaching. For instance, you have mentioned your own coaching of test players by someone like yourself who didn't play first-class cricket. It would appear, therefore, that a coach doesn't have to be a better exponent of a skill than his pupil, in other words, they are fulfilling some other role. Could you comment on that?

JM: Top performers do not automatically become the best, or even good, coaches, just as the best artists, musicians and actors are not always the best teachers of their arts.

There are many examples in sports such as tennis, golf, snooker and boxing where highly respected coaches have never played at the highest level. Nevertheless they are able to develop the skills of top performers within their sport. It is true to say that a good coach who has played at a high level is a great asset and such coaches often become outstanding specialist coaches within their particular field. However, it is also true to say that some high-level performers have neither the patience nor the communication skills to convey their undoubted knowledge to others in a clear, concise and interesting manner.

Coaching therefore, is very much like teaching in that you can have all the knowledge and skill in the world, but this is of little use if you cannot put it over to other people.

TP: So what you are saying is that many leading exponents will not become good coaches because they cannot communicate? Or perhaps because they would become impatient with those of lesser abilities than themselves?

JM: That's right. I think it goes back to patience. Another point is that some tend to coach as they themselves played the game and, as I said earlier, you need to adapt your methods to the person you are coaching because not everybody plays the same way.

TP: We were talking earlier of helping players of much greater ability than yourself to come to terms with their problems. Can you give me an actual example of this?

JM: Over the years many top players come to the School requesting help. Players who are confident in their ability are never afraid to ask for assistance because they understand that sometimes things do go wrong. Whether the coach has played at the same level is not important, provided the player has confidence in the coach.

Personally, I had a most interesting experience with Phil Simmons, the West Indian opening batsman. Phil had been hit by a bouncer against Gloucestershire and it was claimed that he had died on the pitch. Six months later he came to Lord's and asked if he could go on the bowling machine. I took him in the net with the machine and threw balls to him for four hours a day for about three months. At first, as a result of his injury, he displayed a total lack of confidence and belief in himself – in fact, for a whole week all we worked on was the back-foot defensive shot, the ball being put through the machine followed by a little chat as to how he was doing – and gradually his confidence returned. We graduated through the whole range of shots and he was playing with great power and precision.

He returned to the West Indies and resumed his first-class career in the Red Stripe Competition and was soon opening the batting for the West Indies, scoring a hundred in the 1992 World Cup in Australia.

In the past two years he has been back to Lord's on one or two occasions with a request for further assistance.

This serves as an example of how a top level performer can benefit from coaching from someone who has not played at the highest level – playing ability and playing history are not necessarily relevant to how well a person can coach.

TP: Is there an approach to coaching you use? By this I mean, can you elaborate on some of the methods you employ?

JM: I think the most important things are to show enthusiasm and to encourage people. I think it is important to make your coaching session enjoyable to both pupil and coach, and that you appear interested in the performance of the player and not just for one coaching session, but over a period of time.

It is important to give value for money at each session. A good, honest and open feedback is always my aim, together with a genuine interest in the pupil's match play performances.

TP: It all sounds very positive, but are there frustrations in being a coach?

JM: Yes, there are frustrations, such as young people who do not utilize their talent and also qualified coaches who do not use their skills in active involvement with their sport.

TP: And the main satisfactions of being a coach?

JM: The pleasure of doing something you love and the satisfaction of seeing young people succeed and fulfil their potential.

TP: What are the main attributes needed to become a successful coach?

JM: Enthusiasm, plus a caring nature. Patience and the ability to accept that sometimes progress will be slow. The ability to observe, to listen, to diagnose and to provide positive feedback and, perhaps most of all, the ability to gain the best from people.

TP: Are there any pitfalls to avoid, ie, things coaches shouldn't do?

JM: It is very easy to see what people do wrong, and perhaps over-emphasize faults. It is also very easy to coach at the wrong level and sometimes the pupil expects too much too soon. You need to instil patience in pupil and self and have the conviction that with time and practice people will improve. Remember that rates of development vary as does the rate at which people learn. It is easy to forget that and expect too much too soon.

Also, do not pressurize participants and avoid creating anxiety. Coaches should not neglect the less experienced participants and should avoid having favourites.

For some people, the game of cricket is very important and therefore in giving feedback one shouldn't say things that are too harsh. Having said that, of course, one shouldn't tell lies either to overbuild aspirations or kill enthusiasm.

Summary

Some of the main points in this chapter:

- Managers are increasingly taking on a counselling role.
- The range of situations where counselling is required is large. Managers should recognize their own limitations and know when it is appropriate to engage an outsider to assist.
- Counselling offers many benefits to individuals, from helping them address and solve their own problems to assessing their development needs.
- A client-centred approach to counselling is the most effective way to obtain ownership of the problems and a commitment to change.
- Counselling offers many benefits to organizations and can be a significant organizational development vehicle.

- There are many skills involved in being a counsellor and it is important that managers undergo training in counselling skills
- The skills of giving feedback are very important for the modern manager, whose role as a developer is increasing.
- Whereas training is concerned with equipping a person with the basic skills to meet the required standard, coaching is concerned with enabling a person to achieve their potential, which could at best be excellent and at worst, a personal best.
- Coaching is a valuable development vehicle for individuals and organizations, focusing on opportunities rather than problems.
- Managers who become coaches need to be carefully selected and trained.

References and further reading

Burdett, John O (1991) To coach or not to coach – that is the question!' *Industrial and Commercial Training*, 323, 5. Bradford: MCB University Press.

Carkhuff, R (1983) *The Art of Helping*, Amherst: Human Resources Development Ltd.

Couper, D and Stewart, J (1993) *25 Role Plays for Developing Counselling Skills*, Aldershot: Gower.

de Board, R (1983) *Counselling People at Work*, Aldershot: Gower.

Egan, G (1962) *The Skilled Helper*, (2nd edn), Monterey, CA: Brooks/Cole.

McLeod, J (1993) *An Introduction to Counselling*, Buckingham: Open University Press.

Mumford, A (1993) *How Managers Can Develop Managers*, Aldershot: Gower.

Nelson Jones, R (1982) *Theory and Practice of Counselling Psychology*, London: Cassell.

Nelson Jones, R (1993) *Training Manual for Counselling and Helping Skills*, London: Cassell.

Reddy, M (1987) *The Manager's Guide to Counselling at Work*, Leicester: British Psychological Society, and London: Methuen.

Rogers, C (1961) *On Becoming a Person*, London: Constable.

Salisbury, F (1994) *Developing Managers as Coaches. A trainer's guide*, Maidenhead: McGraw-Hill.

Stewart, D (1994) 'Help! I need somebody', *Human Resources*, 14, Summer. London: Martin Leach Publishing.

Whitmore, J (1992) *Coaching for Performance*, London: Nicholas Brearley Publishing.

Chapter 9

Developing Training Skills in Managers

To create a true learning organisation in the fast-paced world of the future, training and development activities have to be performed by practically everyone in the workplace on nearly a daily basis; there's no time to wait for the 'professionals to mount a course or create a programme... A great way to develop future leaders is to rotate them through training roles and keep them active in teaching others, even while they pursue their other business responsibilities. (Rosabeth Moss Kanter, 1994)

In Chapter 2, a range of types of training was outlined: management and supervisory training, a variety of skills training and mandatory training, such as induction, equal opportunities and health and safety. Sometimes these needs are met by attending a public course and sometimes by the company training department, who may resource the course themselves or outsource it and use consultants. As the need and demand for training grows, putting increasing pressure on the limited resources of the training department, then line managers will need to be increasingly involved in the design and delivery of training events. Involvement in training is very developmental for managers – it improves presentation skills, interpersonal skills and group management skills for a start, and in my experience the best way to learn and understand something is actually to teach it. A level of insight and understanding is attained that would rarely be possible in the more passive role of student or delegate.

This chapter will describe some of the key stages and skills that a manager new to training will have to know and acquire. Being suddenly thrown in at the deep end can be a traumatic experience, but if managers are equipped with some basic knowledge, they can achieve training competence fairly quickly and improve their self-confidence both as a trainer and as a person. The reader's attention is also drawn to Chapter 3 which gives a brief outline of relevant learning theories which should influence the design of a training event. For those who wish to study and learn further, additional reading is suggested at the end of the chapter.

What is training?

Megginson and Pedler in the *Developing the Developers* report (1991) conducted in the UK on behalf of the Association of Management Education and Development (AMED) defined training as:

> the relatively systematic attempt to transfer knowledge or skills from one who knows or can do to one who does not know or cannot do.

To be a good trainer, therefore, you must have some expertise, experience and skill in the field in which you are training and, unlike coaching, these will be more developed than those of your trainees. In fact, trainees usually perceive the trainer as an authority on the subject.

Types of training

Two broad categories of training exist:

trainer-controlled; a good example is the lecture
learner-controlled; a good example would be an open learning package or an independent action learning set (see Chapter 5).

Each type of training can take place in various settings, such as the classroom, the laboratory, outdoors, or in the IT room in which sophisticated teaching aids may be used. In the years ahead IT, particularly computers, will be used increasingly in training, so familiarization with the IT, and competence in using it, will become essential for all involved in training.

The role of the trainer

Despite the spread of new and more sophisticated forms of IT, it will never replace training in which there is a trainer : trainee interface. In the traditional situation, the trainer has three main roles: subject expert, method expert, and group manager.

Subject expert

Trainees expect the trainer to know something about the subject in which they are training and usually the trainer knows more or has a greater level of skill than the trainees (unlike the coaching situation, for example). Updating your subject is an important task for the trainer.

Method expert

As will be outlined later in the chapter, there are a number of methods to choose from to help your trainees learn. The trainer should be familiar with most and feel comfortable and competent with a few. Becoming competent with a variety of different methods can form part of a self-development plan for the trainer. The trainer's role is to decide on the most appropriate method to ensure effective and lasting learning for trainees. Training methods have evolved a long way from the 'show, tell, do, check' methodology used by Charles Allen in the USA in 1917 to train 50,000 shipyard workers. This was an expedient method of training a large number of workers. The method consisted of demonstration, instruction, completion of task and assessment, with no attention to process and little attention to group interaction. In other words, it was trainer directed, rather than facilitated. We have now come to recognize that in many situations a more participative style of training will achieve better and more rewarding results; in this case the role of the trainer becomes that of a *facilitator* in which the trainer facilitates the learning and development of the group by the most appropriate method using the resources available.

Group manager

This is the area in which facilitation skills are most obvious. Like the empowered manager (see Chapter 4), facilitators require a high level of interpersonal skills to be able to manage, rather than automatically control a group. Trainers therefore need to be sensitive to group atmosphere and mood as well as to the individuals present. They need to analyse individuals and be aware of group dynamics. This is not acquired overnight – it is a gradual process of learning, but facilitation and working with groups can bring immense personal satisfaction and positive outcomes.

Designing a course

When first asked to design and deliver a course, a multitude of questions go through the mind of the potential trainer – about the trainees, venue, course content, assistance, course materials and so on. In order to clarify thinking that will hopefully lead to successful outcomes, it is important that the trainer plans and conducts the training event in a systematic manner. A six-stage systematic approach to course design, shown in Figure 9.1, is advocated. The six stages are described below.

1. *Define the aims*. This refers to the long-term goals of the course.

2. *Designing learning objectives*. These emerge from the broad aims and are sometimes called performance or behavioural objectives. These usually refer to an end product, ie, what your trainees will be able to do, know or think at the end of a course.

All objectives must be crisp and measurable so it helps to write objectives using specific words such as 'list', 'identify', 'use', 'define', which relate to behaviours that trainees can

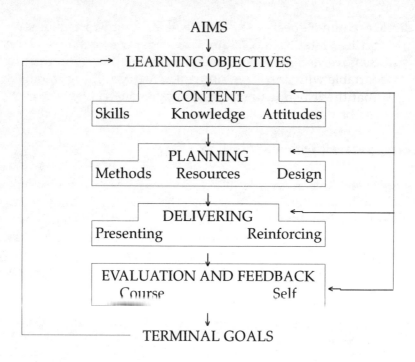

Figure 9.1 *Systematic approach to the development of a course*

display at the end of a course of training. Vague words such as 'show', 'appreciate' and 'understand' should be avoided wherever possible.

3. *Determine the content.* The content is determined from the objectives and so it is useful to start with a rough draft of a course content that will provide participants with the skills, knowledge and attitude change identified in the objectives.

- the cognitive domain of skills we use to collect, know and understand information to gain *knowledge*;
- the psychomotor domain of *skills* we use to programme our actions in order to accomplish tasks; and
- the affective (*attitudes*) domain that affects our attitude to learning and training.

4. *Planning.*

(a) *Choosing the method(s).* There is no one suitable method from the wide range of methods available appropriate for teaching a specific skill. A range of methods will be described later in the chapter. The choice of method should be governed by the method(s) the trainer feels most comfortable with and the resources available, given of course, that the learning objectives and the needs of the trainee are being met in full.

For the trainer, experimentation with different methods is developmental and it is a good way to improve the level of interest in future sessions. The more a trainer can achieve *variety* of method during a training session, the more the chances of the session becoming lively, enjoyable and interesting. In short, variety prevents staleness setting in for both trainer and trainee.

(b) *Determining the resources.* Very rarely are all the required resources available to do the job. That is not to say that trainers have to put up with poor facilities , as modern training rooms in-house and at conference centres and hotels are usually well-equipped. Nevertheless, sophisticated and expensive equipment may not be available, but if it is, it will offer opportunities for varying the method. Whatever the level of experience of the trainer, it is always recommended to be fully aware of resources available before designing a course.

Resources can be divided into two main categories:

- *Physical resources* – include room(s), audio-visual aids and course materials; the latter have to be prepared beforehand.
- *Human resources* – who will be helping you (if anyone) with the course? Do not underestimate the contribution that course members can make to the delivery of a course. Many of the participants will have a wealth of experience which, if tapped, can greatly enrich a training session.

(c) *Designing the course.* Once the aims, objectives, content, methods and resources have been identified, the trainer must begin the final part of the preparation stages, namely the design of the course. This must be done for the whole course and on a session-by-session basis, so that the parts contribute to the whole.

Inexperienced trainers will find that preparing a lesson or session plan will help greatly – it will ensure that the trainer becomes very familiar with the content and at the same time it boosts confidence because it can be a very helpful 'prop' if required.

The session plan is the trainer's guide and script, and a series of them will provide a comprehensive guide to delivering a course. Often these are written up formally to provide a 'Facilitators' guide' which can be used as a resource to help train other managers to deliver a course in the future. A facilitators' guide is usually written after the course has been run several times so that it has been fine-tuned. A tremendous amount of time and effort is initially required to develop and write such guides (along with course materials), but once they have been written, a considerable saving on time results at future courses and it is much easier to train future trainers.

5. *Delivering the course.* If a trainer's preparation has been thorough, the chances of a successful presentation are considerably increased. The old cliché, 'Failing to plan is planning to fail' is certainly true of training events.

At the start of a course it is important to 'tune-in' to a group by checking expectations and existing knowledge or skill levels. In presenting each session it is advisable to:

- err on the side of simplicity and build from this as and when appropriate
- look for individual expertise in the group and use it wherever possible
- try for variety in presentation, using a range of visual aids to enhance and reinforce your message
- keep presentations short; as a rough guide, presentations over 30 minutes should generally be avoided
- allow time for questions and group involvement at the end.

6. *Evaluation of the course.* This is the final stage of the systematic approach and is often neglected, which is foolish. It is just as important as the other stages and it helps determine how effective the learning has been for both trainer and trainee. The evaluation can be carried out by the following methods:

- *tests* to evaluate knowledge and skill acquisition. This gives the trainer and trainee a quantitative assessment of progress made

- *questionnaires* to evaluate the course and the trainer. Response can be used to improve future courses
- *feedback* from trainees and fellow trainers.

The evaluation stage is important for assessing whether learning objectives have been met and also for improving future courses so that learning needs are fully met.

Preparing for a course

An essential part of the preparation is getting ready for the first session. The first session can make or break a course. Good preparation beforehand can again increase the trainer's chances of success. Among the tasks that should be done are:

- ensuring you are familiar with all the material
- ensuring all the training materials are present
- ensuring all visual aids required are present *and* in good working order
- ensuring all arrangements have been made for a good supply of refreshments
- checking that the room has been laid out in the format *you* want.

Room layout

Much training takes place in purpose-built accommodation, but this is not always the case. Whatever the situation, it is recommended that the trainer visits the accommodation *before* the course. In the case of a totally unfamiliar environment, this will help assess suitability, while in other circumstances it will enable the trainer to decide how the room should best be prepared ready for the training event.

There are several ways in which the furniture of a room can be arranged. This will depend on several factors, notably:

- the type of activity to be undertaken. For example, if trainees are working on individual PCs then a table and chair with adequate space is required

- the size of the group
- the amount of interaction between course members required
- the style of the trainer. Certain layouts are more suitable to an informal way of working and others for a more formal way.

Some examples of seating plans and their advantages and disadvantages are shown in Figure 9.2.

The first session

Every course is a new experience for trainer and trainees, so an element of the unknown exists. For some, especially the new, inexperienced trainer, this new situation may be very threatening. It is therefore important for everyone to have a session for getting acquainted. During this session individuals normally share information about themselves to include name, job, objectives in attending and so on. While this activity (usually referred to as an 'ice-breaker') enables much information to be shared, its primary objective is to reduce tension and anxieties because, while they exist an atmosphere will pervade that is neither conducive to learning nor to a good performance by the trainer.

A number of ice-breaking exercises are available. There are no hard and fast rules as to what is the most appropriate nor as to the time that should be spent on them. Timings and choices are very much down to the opinions and expertise of the trainer.

Training methods

The choice of the right method for the task in hand is the job of the professional trainer and is part of the set of skills that must be acquired and developed if becoming a competent trainer is the goal.

Research indicates that learners retain about:

10 per cent of what they read
20 per cent of what they hear

30 per cent of what they see
50 per cent of what they both hear and use
70 per cent of what they say
90 per cent of what they say and do.

Thus trainees retain more of the things they do than of the things they are told. Put another way, trainees retain far more if they participate and are involved than if they are passive. This, therefore, should impact considerably on the choice(s) of methods adopted. Some of the major methods are outlined below.

Lecture

Despite the increasing emphasis in recent years on participative methods, the lecture or presentation is still the most widely recognized and used method in training. Most people can become competent, if not inspired, at presenting. Managers who aspire to senior positions need to become good at presenting and there is no better way to develop good presentation skills than to spend time in training. Good presentation skills are an excellent way of boosting personal credibility whether in training or in any other field. Some tips to help managers become competent at presenting are as follows.

- Establish personal credibility and support with the group at the start.
- Clearly inform the group of the structure of the presentation. This usually means that you 'Tell 'em what you are going to say, tell 'em, then tell 'em what you have told them!'.
- Establish your presence with the group by standing up when talking, but not being statuesque.
- Be aware of the attention span of an audience. Research indicates that during a presentation, attention starts high but drops steadily before returning to the early high, probably because the presenter indicates the end is imminent. Presentations should therefore be short and should not exceed 30 minutes.
- Use visual aids wherever possible. The OHP is almost a must and its regular use will usually raise attention levels as well as reinforcing the message.
- Maintain good eye contact with *all* members of the group.

Classroom-shaped

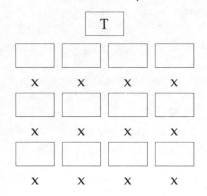

This is one way of accommo-
dating large numbers

• Involves feelings of 'back at
  school'
• Does not encourage interaction and participation

Table layout

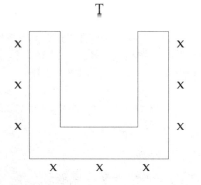

Ideal for groups of less than 20

• Gives learners plenty of
  space
• Allows tutor to move
  freely within the group
• Facilitates use of visual aids
• Promotes discussion
• Allows delegates to do
  much individual work

Boardroom-shaped

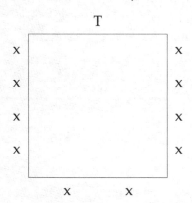

This offers similar advantages
to the previous layout, but does
not allow the tutor to move as
freely within the group

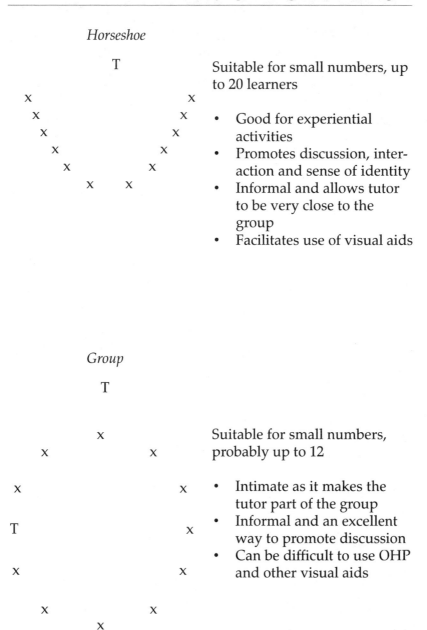

Horseshoe

T

Suitable for small numbers, up to 20 learners

- Good for experiential activities
- Promotes discussion, inter-action and sense of identity
- Informal and allows tutor to be very close to the group
- Facilitates use of visual aids

Group

T

Suitable for small numbers, probably up to 12

- Intimate as it makes the tutor part of the group
- Informal and an excellent way to promote discussion
- Can be difficult to use OHP and other visual aids

Figure 9.2 *Advantages and disadvantages of different seating plans*

- Allow time for questioning; this is usually best done at the end of the presentation rather than during the presentation itself. Regular interruptions for questions during the presentation interrupt the flow of the presentation and may distort the message.
- Remember the figures given earlier about learner retention so, after the presentation, ensure your trainees are 'put into the doing mode'.

Demonstration

Demonstration can either be woven into a lecture or can be carried out on its own. It is a useful method because it links theory and practice, attracts and holds trainees' attention, is very much earthed in the reality of the trainees' world and it gives the trainer the opportunity to establish credibility by demonstrating expertise. Its main drawback is that things can go wrong, especially if you are using complex equipment. The importance of preparation again needs to be emphasized.

Usually, demonstrations should be followed by giving the trainees the opportunity to practise what has been demonstrated by the trainer. The trainer can often improve group management by utilizing the more able members of the group, particularly if resources are limited, and raise individual motivation if the trainees are able to recognize the application of what has been learned to their real-life situation.

Discussion

This method is a good way for managers to develop group management skills which can be transferable to other situations such as chairing meetings. From a training point of view it is a good way of covering the essential points of a session while at the same time giving everyone the opportunity to contribute.

Good discussions are characterized by:

- a good exchange of ideas and information with active involvement of all members of the group;
- contentious issues are confronted;

- ideas and opinions are challenged, but not in a destructive manner;
- the discussion leader exercises firm control of the proceedings if it is required and does not allow members to go off at a tangent or to waste time; and
- the discussion is terminated at an appropriate point.

Managing a discussion successfully requires a group leader with an acute sensitivity to the group and its dynamics which are very different skills and approaches to those required for lecturing and demonstrating. Becoming competent at this is a great confidence-booster and improves interpersonal skills enormously.

Case study

This method has been widely used in management training by the Harvard Business School. Specific details of a problem, usually in written form, are presented to a group of trainees who are asked to arrive at a solution based upon the facts available. It is a very good method for teaching analytical skills and decision making. For trainers, case studies require:

- lengthy preparation time and several trials before they are fully ready. Trainers should always be aware of their immediate reality as a source of material and inspiration for writing case studies;
- clear and concise briefing (written and oral) to participants; and
- good facilitation skills, especially in debriefing and summarizing, so that learning for trainees is maximized.

Role play

This is widely used in skills training – for example in interviewing skills, conducting meetings and customer care courses. Group members are assigned certain roles and required to work through a situation or problem while in role. There is a greater element of risk for the trainer in facilitating role plays because of their unpredictability, but like most situations, the greater the risk, the greater the potential pay-off for participants.

If firmly handled by the trainer, role plays can be enjoyable and stimulating, with a high level of learning. If closed circuit television is used, participants can become acutely aware of their own behaviours and their effect on others. If poorly handled, role plays can degenerate into horseplay with participants exaggerating their perception of role. The result can be that much valuable time is wasted and a cooling-down period may be required before normal training is resumed.

Developing facilitation skills among managers to the extent that they can use methods such as role plays competently, is extremely developmental for managers. It develops their interpersonal and group management skills, particularly in the giving of feedback to individuals. Managers who can do this competently in the training situation will find that giving feedback in the work situation to subordinates at appraisal, from diagnostic instruments or when there is a performance problem, is so much easier and less stressful.

Using visual aids

There are a variety of visual aids available today, but the two most frequently used are the overhead projector (OHP) and the flip-chart.

Overhead projector

These are standard equipment in virtually every training or conference room. If you do not feel confident and competent in using the OHP, your progress in training, and probably management, will be limited. Some tips on its use are as follows.

- Check that the machine is fully operation and focused *before* the presentation.
- Set the screen at an angle for the audience, not straight in front (see Figure 9.3), otherwise the presenter can obscure the view of the audience.
- Have the transparencies to hand in order so that the

changeovers do not interrupt the flow the presentation.
- Have overlays professionally produced if possible, using colour and diagrams as appropriate.
- Face the audience all the time, *not* the screen.
- Obtain a pointer or laser pointer to point to relevant information displayed on the screen.
- Turn the projector off when not in use otherwise a blank screen or an inappropriate slide can distract from the current point.

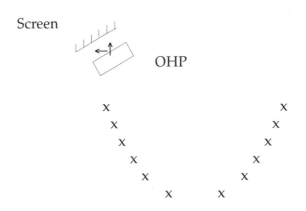

Figure 9.3 *A suggested layout for presenting*

Flipcharts

Like the OHP, flipcharts are standard equipment in every training or conference room. Some tips on their use are as follows:

- write tidily and in large, legible letters
- stand to the side of the flipchart and ensure all members of the audience can see
- use a variety of colours
- if you are building up your presentation on the flipchart, a lightly pre-prepared sketch of relevant material in pencil will act as a very useful *aide-mémoire* – and your audience will be impressed by your memory!

Summary

Some of the main points in this chapter.

* Using line managers in a training role develops management skills in such areas as oral presentation, interpersonal skills, giving feedback and group management.
* Trainers usually have a higher level of knowledge and/or skill than their trainees, although high-level expertise will often exist in some training groups.
* Trainers should have expertise in their subject, the ability to manage a group, and be able to use a variety of methods to help people learn.
* New courses need to be planned beforehand in a careful systematic way.
* All courses need to be evaluated after delivery in order to improve future delivery and learning.
* The layout of a training room can really influence interaction among trainees and the atmosphere within a group.
* Learning methods that are participative will ensure that trainees learn more.
* Trainers should attempt to become competent with a variety of training methods and with a number of visual aids.

References and further reading

Bramley, P (1995) *Evaluating Training Effectiveness. Translating theory into practice*, (2nd edn), Maidenhead: McGraw-Hill.

Kanter, R M (1994) in 'The Future of Workplace Learning and Performance', in *The Past, Present and Future of Workplace Learning*, Alexandria, VA: ASTD.

Megginson D and Pedler, M (1991) *Developing the Developers*, London: Association of Management Education and Development.

Pont, T (1995) *Developing Effective Training Skills*, (2nd edn), Maidenhead: McGraw-Hill.

Powell, L S (1978) *A Guide to the Use of Visual Aids*, London: BACIE.

Rae, L (1992) *The Skills of Training. A guide for managers and practitioners*, (2nd edn), Aldershot: Gower.

Index

Accreditation of Prior
    Learning   22
action learning   76–94
action learning sets   77–8,
    87–9
Alder, Harry   127
Allen, Charles   166
Allied Irish Bank   87
American Society for Training
    and Development   1, 63
Andragogy   50
Apollo   13, 86
Argyris, Chris   56
Armstrong, Neil   29

Bach, Richard   76
Bandler, Richard   128
Beaty, Liz   83
Behaviourism   42–5
Belbin, Meredith   124
Bentley, Trevor   89
blockage concept   119–20
Botkin, Jim   63
Bowen, David   65
brainstorming   128
British Airways   14, 29
British Association of
    Counselling   137
British Standards
    Institute   14
Business Growth Training   22

California Personality
    Inventory   124
Canary Islands   51
Carnaudmetalbox   87

career development   131
Carnevale, Anthony   1
Carnevale, Ellen   1
Casey, David   90, 91
case studies   177
Catell's 16 PF   124
Cheadle, Neville   98
Chiumento, Richard   142
Christ   42
client centred therapy   48–50,
    139
coaching, definitions   148
    benefits   149–52
Coal Board   53
cognitive theories   51–2
Collin, Audrey   96
Comet Group   37–40
Confucius   42
Constable, John   2
Coopers & Lybrand   2
corpus collosum   125
counselling
    definition   137
    benefits   138
    Three Stage Model   142
Coupland, Douglas   68, 117

Darling, Phillip   17, 19
Davis, Stan   63
daVinci, Leonardo   126
Darwin, Charles   43
delegation   66–7
demonstration   176
discussion   176–7
Drucker, Peter   17, 19
Dupont   87

Dupont Centre for
    Creativity   127

Egan, Gerard   139, 143
Einstein, Albert   47, 126
Employee Assistance
    Programmes   142
empowerment   64–73
'Eureka' moments   48, 128
Evans, R   127
experiential learning   52–3

facilitation   89, 91–2, 167
Fayol, Henri   71
Federal Express   66
feedback   146–7
flipcharts   179
Francis, Dave   119
Freud, Sigmund   43, 46

GEC   53
generation X   68
Gibran, Kahlil   90, 91
Gordan's Personal Profile
    Inventory   124
Grinder, John   128

Handy, Charles   2
Harvard Business Review   96
Herriot, Peter   14
Honey, Peter   52, 85
humanistic psychology   42–5
Hunt, John   68
Huxley, Aldous   115

ice-breakers   172
ICI Australia   87
individual training needs   33
Industrial Society/ITEM
    Group Survey   99, 107
Investors in People   22, 35–7
ISO 9000   14, 57

Jefferson, Thomas   47
job exchanges   132
job rotation   133

Kanter, Rosabeth Moss   16,
    164
Kennedy, John F   29
Knowles, Malcolm   50
Kohler, W.   51

lateral thinking   128
Lawler, Edward   65
learner retention   172–3
learning cycle   85
learning logs   122–3
learning styles   53
learning organisation   41,
    60–63
Learning Styles
    Questionnaire   123–4
learning to learn   121–2
lectures   173
left brain   125

Malfait, John   154
Maltz, Maxwell   126
Management Charter
    Initiative   2, 22
Manpower Services
    Commission   148
Margerison, Charles   8, 81
Marshall, Sir Colin   15
Maslow, Abraham   43, 46–8,
    125
MCC Cricket School   154
McCormick, Roger   2
McDonald's   58
McGill, Ian   83
McGregor, Douglas   70
Megginson, David   7, 19, 117,
    165
meritocracy   68

mindmapping 127–8
Minnesota Multiphasic
    Personality Inventory
    124
Mintzberg, Henry 9
Morgan, Gareth 87
Mumford, Alan 52, 85, 121
Myers Briggs Type
    Inventory 124

NASA 86
National Curriculum 45
National Sarghum
    Breweries 87
National Vocational
    Qualifications 22
neuro-linguistic
    programming 128–30

objective setting 30
Occupational Personality
    Questionnaire 124
Open Learning 130
Ornstein, Robert 125
overhead projectors 178–9
outcome thinking 129

PA International Survey 99,
    102, 105, 107
Pavlov, Ivan 43
pedagogy 50
Pedler, Mike 7, 19, 61, 115,
    117, 165
personality tests 124
Peters, Tom 70, 72
Pilkington Glass 87, 97
Pinchot, Elizabeth and
    Gifford 59
Pont, Tony 21
psycho-cybernetics 126

Radley, Clive 154

Redley, Michael 137
Revans, Reg 53, 61, 77, 81
right brain 125
Roche, Gerald 96
role play 177–8
Rogers, Carl 136
Roosevelt, Eleanor 47
Royal Mail 14
Russell, P. 127

Salisbury, Frank 148
scientific management 43,
    56–60, 136
secondments 132–3
self actualization 46–8
self awareness 123–4
Semco, Brazil 66, 72–3
Semler, Ricardo 73
Senge, Peter 62
set adviser 80–81, 89–91
Sheehy Report 16
Skinner, B. F. 43
Smith, R. M. 122
Sperry, Roger 125
strategy formulation 16–18
Stewart, Aileen 70
Stewart, T. A. 64
student-centred teaching 49
Suharto, President 3

Taylor, Frederick 56
Telemactus 96
Team Management
    Index 124
Thatcher, Margaret 23
Theory X 136
Theory Y 70
Thorndike, Edward 43
Towers Perrin 27
TQM 66
Trafalgar House 87, 97
Training Agency 27

Training & Enterprise
    Councils   2, 35
training needs analysis   31–5
Tsu, Lao   42, 123

Ulysses   96

Watson, John   43
Woodcock, Mike   119